University of Puget Sound

*From the Archives:
People, Places, and Stories
(1884–2017)*

Researched and written by
John M. Finney

Edited by Chuck Luce

Copyright 2017

Published at the University of Puget Sound
Tacoma, Washington

ISBN 978-0-692-88608-3

Printed in the United States of America

10 9 8 7 6 5 4 3 2 1

*All photos and images courtesy University of Puget Sound Archives,
unless otherwise credited. Cover photo by Mike Martin.*

Contents

Editor's Preface

Author's Introduction

Faces Behind the Buildings

1.	Anderson-Langdon Hall	1
2.	Collins Memorial Library	7
3.	Gail Pauline Day Memorial Chapel	11
4.	Howarth Hall	17
5.	The Human Resources House	21
6.	Jones Hall	25
7.	Kittredge Hall	29
8.	Army Specialized Training Program	41
9.	McIntyre Hall	49
10.	Memorial Fieldhouse: The Commencement Story	55
11.	The Music Building	59
12.	Puget Sound's Bells and Carillon	65
13.	Regester Hall	75
14.	Seward Hall	79
15.	South Hall	83
16.	Thompson Hall	87
17.	Todd Hall	93
18.	Warner Gymnasium	97

People of Puget Sound

19. Homer Amundsen and Boxing at Puget Sound — 103
20. Coolidge Otis Chapman — 109
21. Edward H. Todd, the Man Who Saved Puget Sound — 117
22. Charles Arthur Robbins — 123
23. Frances Fullerton Chubb — 131
24. Lyle Ford Drushel — 141
25. Students' Army Training Corps — 151
26. Warren Everett Tomlinson — 153

Places of Puget Sound

27. Deep Creek Lodge — 163
28. University Place: the campus that almost was — 179
29. Vienna 1966 and 50 Years of Study Abroad — 191

Personal Stories

30. The Methodist Connection — 199
31. My Life as a Cold War Spy — 203

Puget Sound Historical Record and Reference Items — 209

Sources — 245

Campus Map — 256

Editor's Preface

In 2007 John Finney retired from his job of 31 years as university registrar. Being a man who knows more about Puget Sound than anybody (well, he and George Mills), and also being a man, we have observed, who has never seen a historic artifact he didn't want to find out more about, we were not surprised to hear that he had taken up volunteering in the university archives, sorting through the 50 billion photographs sitting around in brittle old boxes and filing cabinets. The university at that time had only recently appointed a full-time archivist, and its collections were mostly uncatalogued. Any excursion into the those cabinets was like an archaeological expedition, but there was so much interesting stuff in there, and John started digging down through the strata—dusting off photographs and negatives, figuring out what they showed, digitizing them, and posting them in an online collection, A Sound Past. He has, in 10 years of meticulous labor, processed about 7,000 images.

At *Arches*, the college alumni magazine, we'd been observing John's progress, and we also had been thinking for some time about starting a column in the magazine that animated the brick-and-stone facades we walked past every day. Here was Seward Hall, a '70s interpretation of the college's signature Tudor Gothic architecture, but who was Seward, and why is there a building with his named chiseled into the entrance lintel? And so a regular feature in the magazine began, researched and written by Mr. Finney starting in 2008.

Over the years, as the articles accumulated, we realized a significant history of the college and the people who made it what it is today was evolving. These should be collected into a single, easy-access reference volume, we thought. When we proposed the idea to John he was totally game. He updated the stories with information that he'd discovered since their original publication, added photos that we didn't have space for in the magazine, and included sources and a revised version of the quick-reference guide that first appeared in the edition of *Arches* commemorating the 125th anniversary of the University of Puget Sound.

To John, who has resolutely refused any compensation for the hundreds and hundreds of hours he has put into his *Arches* columns and this compilation, our most sincere gratitude and admiration.

And to you, who turns these pages wanting to know more about this remarkable place, we hope you enjoy its stories.

Chuck Luce

Author's Introduction

The stories of Puget Sound are the stories of the people of Puget Sound—the faculty, administrators, students, staff, trustees, and community leaders who have worked since 1888 in successive and intermingled generations to build the distinctive university we know and love today.

One of my last projects as associate dean before retiring in 2007 was working with liaison librarian Elizabeth Knight to carve out an archives work room in Collins Memorial Library. Elizabeth's duties included responsibility for the archives on a one-sixth annual basis. After I retired she invited me to come work in the archives, which I did, as a volunteer. Elizabeth helped to guide me to what has become my ongoing passion, the photograph collection. Each image tells a story that must be dug out, much as a photograph in a family's attic shoebox holds its mysteries when there is no writing on the back.

Elizabeth approached *Arches* editor Chuck Luce—would there be interest in a possible "From the Archives" column? His answer was yes. The stories herein were first published in *Arches* over a nine-year period, spring 2008 through spring 2017. I have attempted to bring the stories up to date. A lot happened at Puget Sound during Ron Thomas' presidency.

For example, Jane Carlin became library director in 2008. That was a game-changer for the archives, which I have watched grow from a musty collection of unorganized materials into the professional operation it is today, with a full-time archivist, a part-time digital collections director, and student employees, some of whom have themselves gone on to careers as professional archivists. The university owes much to Jane, as do I.

Her passion: making the archives an educational resource used in teaching. She accomplished this, with archivist Katie Henningsen at her side.

    I loved being registrar, institutional research director, and associate dean. I had a fulfilling 31-year working career at Puget Sound. But sometimes you have to retire to get your ultimate dream job. Working four mornings each week with the university's online A Sound Past digital images collection and with Chuck Luce and Cathy Tollefson at *Arches* has been my dream job, digging out and telling these stories.

John Finney '67, P'94
My grandmother's writing shack
The Aquarium
Spirit Lake, Idaho
July 1, 2016

Faces Behind the Buildings

1. Anderson-Langdon Hall

No permanent student housing existed at the College of Puget Sound until 1939, although the "Sacajawea Cottage" (a remodeled farmhouse on the site of the current Union Avenue campus) served as housing for up to 18 women from 1924 through 1930. The student body was primarily local in the early years, and most students lived at home. But there were always a few out-of-towners, and their numbers grew as the college increased in stature throughout the Northwest. In those days campus administrators felt obligated to look after women students in particular, so it is no surprise that the first permanent residence hall was built for women.

Groundbreaking for the women's residence hall occurred on February 16, 1938. Among dignitaries present was Washington Secretary of State Belle Reeves, the only woman ever elected to that office. Reeves was also a member of the college's board of trustees.

Construction took up most of 1938. The laying of the cornerstone on October 13 was preceded by a ceremony in Jones Hall auditorium at which the Adelphians sang and Belle Reeves gave an address. During 1938 the college celebrated its 50th anniversary, and the building of the residence hall and the laying of the cornerstone were important events in the ongoing celebration. As construction came to an end, an open house took place on

November 18, 1938. In late January 1939 the first women moved in for spring semester.

The building was named for Agnes Healy Anderson, who gave $35,000 toward the $73,000 cost of the residence. But the naming did not occur in her lifetime. At Mrs. Anderson's request, she was not identified as the donor of the funds until after her death, which occurred on April 6, 1940. When the dormitory opened for business in the spring semester of 1939, it was known simply as the women's residence hall.

On October 16, 1940, the university broke ground for its first student center, Kittredge Hall. That ceremony was followed by the naming and dedication of Anderson Hall. Mrs. Anderson's former private secretary, Katheryn Wilson, drew aside the sheet covering the stone that bears the inscription "Agnes Healy Anderson Hall." Present at this ceremony once again was Washington Secretary of State Belle Reeves.

After World War II the college made the conscious decision to become more residential and to provide more on-campus student housing. Todd Hall for men opened in 1948. Construction of an addition to Anderson Hall began in 1953. Years later this addition would be called Langdon Hall. The addition was built with funds borrowed from the federal government at low interest rates under a loan program to universities for defense-related housing. The College of Puget Sound had an ROTC program, and therefore qualified to borrow money under this program. Perhaps students who later lived in Langdon Hall would be surprised to know that their dorm rooms were part of the country's defense efforts. The college applied for a $250,000 loan. When told by the government that the amount requested was too low, the college amended its request to $300,000. The addition actually cost $293,900 and housed 145 women.

On November 14, 1954, an open house was held for the completed addition to Anderson Hall. At about this same time, President R. Franklin Thompson met Myrtella C. Langdon while he was serving as interim pastor of Seattle's Plymouth Congregational Church. Mrs. Langdon was very much interested in supporting her church, the YWCA, and, as a result of her friendship with President Thompson, the College of Puget Sound. Her subsequent gift was used to help pay back the government loan the college had taken out to construct the Anderson Hall addition. The addition was then named Langdon Hall, although the two halls together continued to be known as Anderson Hall in popular campus parlance for several more years. The 1961 *Tamanawas* is the first in which "Anderson-Langdon Hall" replaced "Anderson Hall" as the designation for the two women's residence halls. Today Anderson-Langdon houses both men and women.

In order to conform with city building codes related to earthquakes, Langdon Hall was constructed as a separate building from Anderson, even though the college originally proposed that the north wall of Anderson, being 12 inches thick, would serve admirably as the south wall of the addition without the need for a new wall. At the city's insistence a new wall was built, 18 inches thick, so that the wall between Anderson and Langdon halls is 30 inches of reinforced concrete.

Faces Behind the Buildings

Students by the campus cornerstone and Anderson Hall, circa 1947. The cornerstone now rests at the northwest corner of Kilworth Chapel.

Anderson Hall groundbreaking, February 16, 1938. From left to right: E.L. Blaine; William J. Millard; Mrs. Edward H. Todd; Washington Secretary of State Belle Reeves, wielding the shovel; George A. Smiley; D.J. Young; and President Edward Todd.

The inscription above the southeast door of Anderson Hall, seen here in 1938, exists to this day.

Katheryn Wilson, left, close associate of Mrs. Anderson, unveils the name of Agnes Healy Anderson Hall on October 16, 1940.

Faces Behind the Buildings

2. Collins Memorial Library

When the College of Puget Sound moved to its current location in the fall of 1924, the north half of the basement of Jones Hall served as the college library. There it remained for the next 30 years. But from the beginning CPS President Edward Todd foresaw the need for a separate library building, and in this pursuit he had a friend in longtime trustee and benefactor Everell Stanton Collins.

Collins, a second-generation lumberman, was born in Cortland, New York, in 1866. Everell's mother, a dedicated Methodist, passed her deep religious commitment on to her son, who played critically important roles in the development of two Northwest colleges—Willamette and Puget Sound. President Todd and Everell Collins were in conversation about a new library when, in 1940, Everell died suddenly of pneumonia. Everell's unsigned will left CPS $500,000 to construct the library. But the will that governed disposition of Everell's estate included only $100,000 for the library. Everell's son, Truman Wesley Collins, shared his father's vision and love for the College of Puget Sound. Truman became a personal friend and admirer of Edward Todd's successor, R. Franklin Thompson. Although he was not bound to do so, Truman Collins saw to it that the college received the half-million dollars for the library. Appreciative CPS students honored him with a standing ovation at the April 14, 1953, groundbreaking for Collins Memorial Library.

Architect Silas Nelsen began work in the 1940s on designs for the library. It took him quite some time to deliver a design that President Thompson felt was appropriate for the campus. Nelsen's original design was "a rather oblong building without too much decoration." Thompson insisted that the library had to be "beautiful as well as practical and useful." President Thompson himself contributed to the building's design. He had studied at Oxford and at his suggestion a tower was added, based on the interior tower of Oxford's Magdalen College. Today the tower houses the Howard R. Kilworth Memorial Carillon, a 1954 gift from Howard's brother, William W. Kilworth, for whom Kilworth Chapel is named.

The library was completed early in 1954. On Thursday, April 8, students, faculty, staff, and alumni moved 45,000 books from Jones Hall to the new Collins Memorial Library. Library director Warren Perry borrowed book carts from several libraries in the region so that all of the books could be moved in one day. Dean John Regester canceled classes and, after the books were moved, students departed for spring vacation. A tent tunnel was constructed between Jones Hall and the new library to protect the books in the event of rain. It did rain, and the tunnel saved the day. *The Seattle Times'* Sunday, May 9, 1954, Color Rotogravure Pictorial section contains a five-page story on the book move, accompanied by 12 photographs.

Collins Memorial Library was built to hold 80,000 volumes. At first the library contained faculty and student lounges. But after 20 years of adding to the collection, all of the available space was filled. In 1974 a new $2.7 million wing was dedicated, quintupling the library's capacity for growth. The second floor of the new addition housed classrooms and faculty offices until 2000, when Wyatt Hall opened and Collins Memorial Library received a major renovation.

Everell Collins died 14 years before the library named in his memory opened. Had Truman Collins not honored his father's intent, the library would not have been built as it was when it was. And as a historical footnote relevant to an ideal of today's University of Puget Sound, Truman Collins was among the first to champion the practice of sustainable logging methods. Sustainability continues to the present day as the operational philosophy and practice of The Collins Companies, headquartered in Portland, Oregon. Collins Companies' forests meet criteria of the Forest Stewardship Council for timber sustainability, forest ecosystem maintenance, and socioeconomic benefits to the community.

Puget Sound President R. Franklin Thompson and 1954–1955 ASCPS President James Nelson '55, M.A. '63 wheel a cart of books from the old library in the basement of Jones Hall to the new Collins Memorial Library on April 8, 1954. A tent tunnel was constructed along the route to protect books from the rain.

Faces Behind the Buildings

Library at the north end of the basement of Jones Hall, 1924 or 1925.

Collins Memorial Library under construction, late 1953 or early 1954.

3. Gail Pauline Day Memorial Chapel

When C.H. Jones Hall opened in 1924, almost every college activity took place in that building. The College of Puget Sound was hard-core Methodist in those days, and religious activities were important in everyday college life. Built into Jones Hall was a chapel, located on the second floor in the southeast quadrant of the building. The October 1924 issue of the quarterly college bulletin contains a photograph of the chapel with this caption: "This is our 'Little Church.' It is so constructed that every appointment is conducive to worship. Vesper services are held here Sunday afternoons. Other religious exercises, meditation, and prayer are in order here."

The chapel was dedicated on June 7, 1925, as part of a baccalaureate service two days before the entirety of Jones Hall was dedicated. The chapel was presented by Horace J. Whitacre, chair of the trustees' building committee, with these words: "… we present unto you this chapel, to be dedicated for meditation and prayer and for worship and service of Almighty God in this college."

For the next 25 years the chapel was known as The Little Chapel. It contained an oak reading desk and chair which, according to President Edward Todd, were "used by every president of this institution." President Todd also relates in his history of the college how Mr. and Mrs. William Seymour, during their travels in Europe, became enamored with Holman Hunt's 1854 painting "The Light of the World," which hangs in St. Paul's Cathedral in London. The Seymours loved the painting so much they hired an artist to copy it. Eventually, admiring the College of Puget Sound's Little Chapel, the Seymours presented the oil painting to the college during the 1927–28 academic year. "The Light of the

World" has hung in the chapel ever since. This large painting was for many years an item of interest in the community and attracted many visitors, with its elaborate gold frame containing the words "Behold, I stand at the door and knock; if any man hear my voice, and open the door, I will come in to him, and will sup with him, and he with me. — Revelation 3:20"

One of the students who used The Little Chapel was Gail Pauline Day, who graduated from the College of Puget Sound in 1937. In 1939, while engaged in graduate studies at Northwestern University, Gail Day's life ended tragically at the hands of a drunk driver. On June 7, 1950, with the support of Gail Day's parents, Edward Vernon Day and Grace Nolan Day, The Little Chapel was dedicated to the memory of Gail Day and became the Gail Pauline Day Memorial Chapel, or as it is commonly known, Gail Day Chapel.

Five years earlier, Gail Day's sister, Doris Jean Day '41, was married in the chapel to her husband, Allan Norwood Sapp. Their son, Allan D. Sapp '78, served the college as a trustee. On April 27, 1951, SPURS, the longtime (1925–2006) college sophomore women's service honorary, initiated Lucille Thompson as an honorary member of SPURS in Gail Day Chapel. (Lucille, beloved by students, was wife of President R. Franklin Thompson.) These and hundreds of other marriages and ceremonies occurred in The Little Chapel and Gail Day Chapel.

By the 1970s Jones Hall was bulging at the seams. Covetous eyes were cast increasingly on the precious space occupied by a chapel in what was becoming less an all-purpose building and more an administrative one. The university's first full-time chaplain, the Rev. K. James Davis, was shown Gail Day Chapel in Jones Hall when he interviewed for the position in the spring of 1977. When he showed up for work in the fall, he was astonished at his inability to locate the chapel. During the summer of 1977 Gail Day Chapel had been moved quickly, quietly, and with no fanfare from Jones Hall to Kilworth Chapel. The Jones Hall space it occupied was then converted to offices for expanding university relations operations. Most of the university community understood the reason for the move, although some missed the old Gail Day Chapel enormously.

In Kilworth, Gail Day Chapel occupied converted storage space behind the chancel until 1989, when that space was needed for the pipe organ built and installed by Paul Fritts '73. Gail Day Chapel then moved to its current location in the northwest corner of the second floor of Kilworth Chapel. Today, Gail Pauline Day Memorial Chapel is a nice space that remains "open to the campus community daily for meditation and prayer for persons of all religious convictions." The copy of Hunt's "The Light of the World" still hangs in Gail Day Chapel, but without its elaborate gold frame.

Gail Pauline Day '37, for whom Gail Pauline Day Memorial Chapel is named.

Faces Behind the Buildings

As did hundreds of others over the decades, a bride waits with her father to enter the Little Chapel from the second floor of Jones Hall on October 10, 1945. The bride is Doris Jean Day '41 and her father is Edward Vernon Day. Five years later the Little Chapel was dedicated to the memory of Doris' sister, Gail Day '37.

Gail Pauline Day Memorial Chapel

Wedding in the Jones Hall Little Chapel of Doris Jean Day '41 and Allan Norwood Sapp, October 10, 1945, with President R. Franklin Thompson officiating.

Students meditate in Gail Day Chapel, 1955. A copy of the William Holman Hunt painting "The Light of the World" hangs above.

Faces Behind the Buildings

4. Howarth Hall

Howarth Hall was Puget Sound's first science building, a function it filled for 44 years. Construction of Science Hall began in 1924, the same year Jones Hall was finished. But, whereas Jones Hall was completed in just one year, Science Hall remained unfinished until 1927. For lack of funds to complete the building, Science Hall construction was halted with just the basement in use until additional funds were borrowed and construction resumed. The lintels over the west and north doors read "Physical Sciences."

The college faced an $80,000 debt on Science Hall, a considerable sum. In 1930 Leonard Howarth, president of the St. Paul and Tacoma Lumber Company, died. He left $150,000 "to be used for the benefit of the city." College of Puget Sound President Edward Todd suggested the college apply for the entire amount. Some, including the college's attorney, doubted the city could give any money to a private, denominational college. But the attorney discovered that a group appointed by Leonard Howarth's brother, William, would decide the use of the funds, not the city council. So application was made and, in January 1932, the college received $125,000 of the Howarth money to be used to repay the Science Hall debt and to provide for scholarships. On Founders' and Patrons' Day, February 19, 1932, Science Hall was dedicated and its name was changed to Leonard Howarth Hall, eight years after construction began. On that day "Leonard Howarth Hall" replaced "Physical Sciences" over the north entrance door off Sutton Quadrangle. The lintel over the west door still to this day reads "Physical Sciences."

Faces Behind the Buildings

One of the conditions of the Howarth bequest was that "a suitable portrait of Leonard Howarth be hung in Science Hall." The portrait, unveiled at the February 19, 1932 dedication, was painted by 27-year-old Rowena Clement Lung, an instructor in the college's art department. Rowena Lung later married biology professor Gordon Alcorn.

Until 1942, when Puget Sound's first student center, Kittredge Hall, opened, The Commons student dining hall was located in Howarth Hall's basement. Howarth Hall continued to serve as the college's science building until Thompson Hall opened in 1968. The psychology department was then housed in Howarth Hall until 2011, when Puget Sound's new health sciences building, Weyerhaeuser Hall, opened. For several years until the ceramics building was put up in 1971, Howarth basement was home to the art department's ceramicists. Today Howarth Hall houses the education program and several administrative and student services offices.

Puget Sound art instructor Rowena Clement Lung stands by her portrait of Leonard Howarth on the day of its unveiling at the dedication of Leonard Howarth Hall, February 19, 1932. The painting has hung in the Howarth Hall foyer ever since.

Howarth Hall

View from the front steps of Jones Hall of the processional on the front steps of Science Hall on the day of its dedication as Leonard Howarth Hall, February 19, 1932. Note the paper banner covering the new name "Leonard Howarth Hall."

Howarth Hall and the campus cornerstone, September 1964.

Faces Behind the Buildings

5. The Human Resources House

The Civil Rights Act of 1964 forbade employment discrimination based on race, color, national origin, religion, and sex. In January 1972 Congress amended the act to include employees of educational institutions. In March 1972 Puget Sound established a personnel department to ensure compliance with the act.

President R. Franklin Thompson asked Mary Louise Curran '36 to be the department's first director. At the time of her appointment Mary was the college's dean of women and associate director of admission.

The personnel department was housed from the beginning in the white house at 1218 North Lawrence Street on the corner of Lawrence and North 13th streets. The house was given to the college by one Mr. Mullins and was known as Mullins House.

Mary Thompson Turnbull, daughter of former President Thompson, confirms as truth what had become campus lore. That is that Mr. Mullins, known privately by President Thompson and his daughters Mary and Martha as "Moon" Mullins, from the comic strip of the day, gave the house to the college out of affection for "Doc T."

Mr. Mullins, it is said, liked to frequent the Sixth Avenue bars. Often at the 2 a.m. closing time Mr. Mullins was unable to navigate his way home unaided. When the bartender or Mr. Mullins himself telephoned President Thompson for help, "Doc T" always provided it. Out of gratitude for delivering him safely home on a regular basis over a number of years, Mr. Mullins declared that someday he would give his house to the college. And that he did.

Mary Curran worked fast after becoming personnel director in March 1972. In May she hired Lynda Lott as assistant director. Later she hired a second assistant director, William Frey. By July the trustees had approved an affirmative action program for the college. By October the personnel department had taken over, from the financial vice president, responsibility for maintaining staff and faculty health insurance records. Mary drafted the college's first employees' manual by the end of the year. By April 1973 the personnel department had become responsible for administering the college's OSHA paperwork and the unemployment compensation program. And by 1974 a personnel classification program was in place to help ensure equitable salaries and benefits across similar types of jobs. All of these accomplishments and more are described by former director Rosa Beth Gibson in her written history of the department.

In her capacity as personnel director Mary Curran also served as affirmative action officer for the college. Mary was very much interested in increasing the number of women and minorities hired in staff and faculty positions.

When Mary retired in 1976, Lynda Lott took over as the second director of personnel. Rosa Beth Gibson became its third director in 1977, serving for 34 years before retiring in 2011. Rosa Beth was a calming guide as she led the department through a maze of ever more complex institutional and governmental expectations to make it the professional operation that it is today. The department's fourth leader, Cindy Matern, carries the tradition forward.

During summer 1994, professional jargon caught up with the college when personnel became "human resources," and the office was renamed the human resources department. The role of director expanded to oversee student employment, and career and employment services, and the title was changed to associate vice president.

The partnership between Mullins House and the personnel/HR department came to an end in summer 2011 when, anticipating construction of Thomas Hall (known as Commencement Hall 2013–2016), the department moved to the basement of Howarth Hall after the psychology department moved to Weyerhaeuser Hall. In June 2012, Mullins House was razed.

The house at 1218 N. Lawrence, for nearly 40 years the university personnel department office, was removed in June 2012 to make way for construction of Commencement Hall, renamed Thomas Hall in 2016. The "1218" address plate visible to the left of the front door was carved by the personal department's first director, Mary Wortman Curran '36, P'61,'67 after she retired.

Faces Behind the Buildings

6. Jones Hall

The words "Jones Hall" are spoken many times each day on campus and each invocation honors the memory of civil war veteran and lumberman Charles Hebard Jones, born April 13, 1845, in East Randolph, Vermont. In 1851 Charles moved with his family to Wisconsin, where he attended Lawrence University before enlisting in 1864 in Company D, 41st Wisconsin Infantry. In 1872 Charles married Franke M. Tobey. The couple eventually came to Tacoma, where Charles was one of the founders of the St. Paul and Tacoma Lumber Company.

May 22, 1923, was a momentous day in the history of the College of Puget Sound. On that day the entire faculty and student body processed together from the campus at Sixth and Sprague streets to a vacant field centered at North 15th and Warner streets. There Mrs. Franke M. Jones pledged $180,000 toward construction of the new campus. The trustees accepted the pledge, and Jones Hall groundbreaking took place immediately. Taking turns at the groundbreaking plow were Mrs. Jones, President Edward Todd, construction contractor J.E. Bonnell, and many students. Mrs. Jones' gift, together with her husband's earlier pledge of $20,000, was used to build Jones Hall, named in memory of her husband, who had died in 1922. Charles and Franke were married for 50 years.

May 22, 1923, was selected by President Edward Todd for the groundbreaking ceremony because that day was Mrs. Jones' 78th birthday. For many years thereafter May 22 was celebrated annually as Campus Day, and flowers honoring Mrs. Jones' birthday were placed in the Jones Hall entranceway beneath the plaque dedicating the building to her husband's memory.

Faces Behind the Buildings

Charles Hebard Jones and Franke Tobey Jones on their 26th wedding anniversary, Menominee, Michigan, June 25, 1898.

Jones Hall, from the basement roof of the unfinished Science Hall (renamed Howarth Hall in 1932), 1925.

Jones Hall

Jones Hall under construction, February 12, 1924.

On the Jones Hall steps, the first assembly of faculty and students on the new campus, September 17, 1924. Franke Tobey Jones stands in the front row, third from right, between President Edward Howard Todd (whose handwritten inscription appears on the face of the photograph) and his wife, Florence Anne Moore Todd.

Faces Behind the Buildings

7. Kittredge Hall

Imagine September 1941. You are back on campus for your sophomore year. You move into Anderson Hall, perhaps, or into one of the approved off-campus residences for men, then head for Jones to check on your classes at the registrar's office. Because you are a sophomore now, you enter Jones through the front door—you weren't allowed as a freshman. Things are looking up.

Almost everything that happens on campus takes place in Jones—most classes, for example. Jones is full of classrooms and faculty offices. The administration—president, dean of the college, dean of women, bursar, and registrar—don't take up much space.

Then there are all the clubs and organizations that meet in Jones and all the social events. You're a member of the International Relations Club, you'll help ASCPS student government put the *Log Book* together, and you belong to Pi Kappa Delta debate honorary. The groups meet wherever you can find a cubbyhole and sometimes you have to go off campus.

And ASCPS and the *The Trail* and *Tamanawas* offices—also in Jones. The bookstore's in the basement. Weekly chapel (attendance required) is in Jones auditorium, and then there is a real chapel—called The Little Chapel—on the second floor. A great thing about Jones, though, is the student telephone. If you need to call someone, your $7.50 student activity fee includes the privilege of using the phone in *The Trail* office. Sure isn't very private, though.

Oh, and don't forget the college library. It's in Jones basement. Not open on Sundays. And the third and fourth floors—mostly art galleries.

Of course, Howarth Hall is jammed up too, and you head over for lunch. Coming up the steps of Jones as you leave is Dr. Todd, and you say hello. At first you thought he was stern and gruff, but he isn't really. He sure is old, though—79. He was tough when he had to be to save the school back in the olden days. But now he's a sweetie, in his last year, going to retire at the end of spring. Just think—29 years as president, hard to imagine. You guess you're really going to miss the guy.

You march right up the front steps of Howarth—you couldn't do that as a freshman either. Here's where all the science classrooms and labs are, and on the top floor is the natural history museum. Most important right now, though, is The Commons in the basement, where students eat their meals. It costs you $18 a month to eat in The Commons. What do they think you are made of, money? And that's in addition to your room and the $175 tuition for the year. Man!

Nice to know, though, that if you get sick you can go see Dr. Hermann or Dr. Sleep in the medical office on the second floor of the gym. They hang out there every weekday afternoon for one whole hour, 12:30 'til 1:30. You wonder if Dr. Sleep ever prescribes sleep—probably the cure for most student ailments.

Yup, the campus sure is crowded. All the faculty and more than 600 students are crammed into Jones and Howarth and the gym and the old music conservatory. The only dorm is Anderson Hall, and you have to be a girl to live there. That's it—that's the whole campus—five buildings.

After lunch you wander down to see how number six is coming along—the new student center. You feast your eyes on it—man, it looks big. Really—this whole building for the students? Amazing! You get excited at the thought. The bookstore will move to the student center—it'll be on the ground floor just to the right as you enter from Lawrence Street. Wow, look at that cute little bay window up there on the second floor—that's where Dean Drushel's apartment will be. She's dean of women, and she'll be in charge of the whole building. She's so great. You heard that there will even be a couple of rooms for girls to live in and a room in the basement for a couple of guys.

You go up to the building and look in one of the windows—they sure made a lot of progress over the summer. You can see almost all the way across the interior of the building. That'll be The Commons, moving over from Howarth, and it'll be huge, open to skylights on the roof, with a big balcony all the way around on the second floor, where you can look down onto all the students hanging around there—magnificent!

And all those rooms on the second floor—for ASCPS, *The Trail*, *Tamanawas*, the YWCA group, Kappa Phi—wow. And the chapter rooms, don't forget about the sorority chapter rooms. You heard that just the other day Professor Tomlinson's daughter Barbara drew names out of a hat that assigned a specific room to each of the four sororities.

You and your friends spent a lot of time last spring downtown "selling bricks" to merchants and anyone you could buttonhole to raise money for this building. A "brickskrieg," they called it. Oh gosh, you don't like to think about the awful things going on in Europe—it seems so far away, but you're worried. The U.S. isn't in it yet, but it seems inevitable. Anyway, the "brickskrieg" raised a lot of money—about $9,000, not an insignificant percentage of the $57,000 total cost of the building. You feel good about that.

On November 14 you are there for the laying of the cornerstone, when Dr. Todd announces that the building will be named Kittredge Hall, for a guy named John M. Kittredge. You aren't sure who he was—later you hear that he never even set foot on the campus. But he gets his name on the building because his daughter gave a bunch of money in his memory. You guess that's OK, but you think about old Senator Davis—professor of history Walter S. Davis—and the more than 400 students and faculty who signed a petition to name the new student center Davis Hall. You call him "Senator" because he *was* one for a long time, in the Washington State Legislature. Man, if it hadn't been for Senator Davis, a lot of the school's early history might have been lost. He wrote about it back in 1907. Hard to believe he's still alive and kicking. But Dr. Todd said the building couldn't be built without the Kittredge money. Oh, well, it'll be worth it. We'll name some other building Davis Hall.

When you return to campus after Christmas vacation things are really different. Because of Pearl Harbor. Everybody is on edge, your worst fears come true. The country is at war with Japan and with Germany. A lot of the guys didn't even come back to school, they just signed up.

But your spirits lift when you see that Kittredge Hall is finished! You hear that over Christmas a whole bunch of people worked hard to move all of the gas stoves and kitchen equipment from Howarth to the new student center.

You go inside and walk around. Beautiful! Upstairs you hear Jim Paulson—he's student body president—giving an impromptu tour and you join the group.

"Look at all these fabulous wood walls. Dr. Todd sure is smart—this stuff's called plywood, something new, and Dr. Todd got some manufacturers to donate it—told 'em Kittredge would be 'a lumberman's showcase.' Get it? We're the Loggers, after all. There's 18 different kinds of plywood in this building. Isn't it neat?

"But hey, I want to show you my favorite room in the whole place. Follow me." You all troop downstairs and walk through The

Commons to the southeast corner of the building, and there it is. "See that? We have our own, genuine soda fountain—a snack bar, where you can get a hamburger any old time. Isn't it great? We don't need to go off campus anymore just to get a milkshake." You marvel at the green stools all around the counter. Fantastic.

The group re-enters The Commons, and you stop and stare. This one big room extends from one end of the building all the way to the other end, north to south. And between the two big windows at the north end is a fireplace that Jim tells you cost $500, just for that one fireplace. You notice the carpeting and the plush sofa and chairs, and Jim demonstrates how sliding doors close off the whole north end to become a really nice student lounge.

Over the next few days Kittredge fills with students and with faculty, too, and—before you know it—is the social heart and activity center of the campus, like a beehive. When Kittredge is officially dedicated on January 16, 1942, the whole campus is opened up for inspection and you help lead tours of the buildings.

At the end of spring term Dr. Todd retires. One of the most popular students on campus, his granddaughter Ruth Pauline Todd, graduates—she was this year's *Tamanawas* editor. But there were some students who should've graduated but didn't—your pals of Japanese ancestry. Seniors, juniors, sophomores, freshmen— three dozen in all—hauled off to camps, even though they were U.S. citizens, the nicest kids you could ever hope to meet. It made you cry, and it still does.

A new man, R. Franklin Thompson, is introduced as Puget Sound's 10th president. You can't believe how young he looks compared to Dr. Todd. Dr. Thompson—you come to call him "Doc T"—is only 34 years old. You look at him hopefully, and you cannot even begin to imagine how much energy he has.

It's September 1943, and you return to Puget Sound for your senior year. Martha Lucille is born October 25 to "Doc T" and Mrs. Thompson and is immediately "adopted" by the students. Kittredge Hall has been part of the fabric of campus life for almost two whole years now. The new student center has made a huge difference to the college. Where before student groups were scattered all over the place, there is now a central place—a center—to come to. Paths are worn in the grass from all points of the compass leading to Kittredge. School spirit is high—except for the war, of course. Enrollment is half what it was, fewer than 300, with so many of the guys, including faculty, away fighting.

In October comes word that Puget Sound has been selected to host one of the country's Army Specialized Training Units, number 3966, for the training of soldiers in engineering. The campus scrambles to accommodate the 238 men who will arrive in December. Enrollment will double, overnight.

The gym is established as housing for the soldiers. They call it "the barn." Some of the lucky ones live in "the palace"—Kittredge Hall, unit headquarters. The Commons becomes off-limits to regular students except for the snack bar. The sororities give up their beautiful chapter rooms, and all student activities disperse across campus once again. But you and the others vacate your wonderful Kittredge Hall with the knowledge that you are contributing to the war effort.

In fact it seems that everyone on campus, including you, welcomes the soldiers with open arms. You serve on the war coordination committee to promote smooth relations between campus and Army. You hear that some of the girls have set up a "date bureau committee," now that men are once again present in reasonable ratio. All of this takes place with Dean Drushel's guidance, of course. The soldiers integrate easily, and they reinvigorate the campus.

Your last semester begins: spring 1944. You learn why much later (it's because of the buildup to the D-Day invasion) but, disappointing for you and the whole campus, the ASTP units across the country are called up from their college homes to prepare to fight. Puget Sound's soldiers leave in March. They were with you only three months. As they leave, you realize they are part of the heart and soul of the school and of Kittredge Hall and will be always. You pray for them.

You graduate, and over the years you return to campus as often as you can for Homecoming. You are always reminded of the excitement you felt as a student when Kittredge Hall opened. Your very own student center—it symbolized in bricks and mortar a promise to you and to all students that this small college was really going places.

After the war enrollment explodes, and Kittredge Hall, perfect for 600 students, is inadequate for 2,000. In late 1959 a new student center opens across the street. Kittredge Hall becomes the home of the art department. You walk around. The Commons is now an art gallery. A ceiling over the gallery creates second-floor space for art studios. The old student lounge is a small art gallery. Later on the fireplace is covered up, but you smile knowingly—it is still there, an archaeological treasure waiting to be discovered and perhaps restored someday.

You understand that Kittredge isn't a student center anymore. And you see that it is still plenty busy and well used. The second floor corner rooms aren't sorority chapter rooms. But they are alive with the energy of students engaged in artistic expression. You feel that Kittredge is still a great place—it still has spirit.

Faces Behind the Buildings

January 2017: Getting around is more difficult for you now, but you return to campus for the 75th anniversary of the opening of Kittredge Hall. The campus is off-the-charts spectacular these days—hard to believe there were only five buildings your freshman year. Man, you would love to stroll the grounds arm in arm with Dr. Todd and show him what the campus has become. And Kittredge—you love the place as much as ever. It was a student center for only 18 of its 75 years, but you were there at the beginning. You know what it meant.

Students converse outside John M. Kittredge Hall, 1947. The dormer window identifies the living room of the dean of women's apartment. Lyle Ford Drushel was dean of women, 1931–1953.

Kittredge Hall

Kittredge Hall in 1947. The bricked over "doorway" on the south side was not the result of a renovation. It was like that from the beginning; the architect intended the archway for visual balance.

Students with the new Log board outside Kittredge Hall listing late spring semester student activities, including Campus Day and the annual May Day Festival, circa 1950.

Faces Behind the Buildings

Puget Sound students welcome ASTP soldiers outside their Kittredge Hall headquarters, December 1943.

The noontime lunch crowd in the Kittredge Hall Commons, seen from the balcony, 1949. This view faces south, toward North 15th Street. The three open doors on the balcony are The Trail/Tamanawas office far right and two sorority chapter rooms.

Kittredge Hall

Bookstore Manager Lela "Shifty" Schiffbauer, second from right, and student employees wait on student customers, 1949. The bookstore was located in the southwest corner of the ground floor.

The student lounge at the north end of The Commons was a popular student gathering place. With a fire in the fireplace, it was cozy indeed. This February 1952 image shows a discussion session held during the annual Religious Life Emphasis Week.

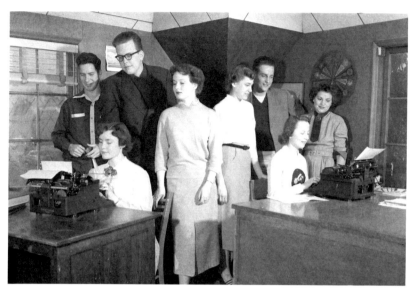

Students work on the 1953 edition of Tamanawas. Standing; Jack Cranfill, Scott McArthur, Diane Seeley, Lynn Green, Tom Lennon, and Mary-Jane Engoe. Seated; Billie Shively and Evalyn Emert.

Students roast marshmallows in the student lounge fireplace, 1953.

8. Army Specialized Training Program

When World War II veteran Cole Barnard visited Puget Sound with his daughter, Liz Herdman, during Homecoming and Family Weekend in Oct. 2016, he asked especially to visit an old haunt of his, Kittredge Hall. Cole was one of 238 army privates enrolled at Puget Sound from Dec. 1943 to March 1944 in the Army Specialized Training Program (ASTP), unit 3966, Major Darlington and Captain Smith in charge. Headquarters was Kittredge Hall.

Kittredge was the campus' first student center. Students loved the place and used it heavily from the beginning. But Pearl Harbor brought the country into the war, and soon Puget Sound enrollment was almost halved as students enlisted or were drafted. In 1943 the U.S. Army, anticipating eventual victory in the war, created the ASTP to train soldiers in the skills necessary to re-establish order and infrastructure in occupied territory. Some 150,000 soldiers were enrolled in three-month ASTP courses at more than 200 colleges across the country. Unit 3966 was to train engineers.

Kittredge Hall was given over to house officers and soldiers for the duration of their stay. Puget Sound students viewed the giving up of their wonderful new student center as a contribution to the war effort. The soldiers arrived early in December to begin what the army designated as Term 1 of Curriculum B-1, running from Dec. 13, 1943, through March 4, 1944. Term 1 courses were chemistry, English, geography, history, mathematics, and physics, a grueling schedule. Subsequent three-month terms were expected to follow but they did not. Most of the ASTP programs across the country were terminated at the end of Term 1, with a few in medicine continuing. In the buildup to the invasion of Europe the army needed more leaders and infantrymen, and the ASTP was a source of both.

While they were at Puget Sound, the soldiers doubled the student population and revitalized the campus. But everyone understood that the army guys were soldiers first and students second. Their leader, Major Darlington, organized Unit 3966 "as a provisional battalion of two companies," Company A—housed in Kittredge Hall, "the palace," and Company B—housed in the gymnasium (today known as Warner Gym), "the barn." Although all the soldiers were army privates, Major Darlington appointed some of them as acting officers. Cole Bernard was in Company B, consisting of two platoons. He was leader of the first platoon as acting first lieutenant. Beneath him were acting sergeants and acting corporals. Rank insignia could be worn only on the campus, not off campus.

Life was regimented for the soldiers in ways that restricted most socializing to the weekends. Company B marched at attention from the gym to Kittredge for meals except on Sundays and holidays. Soldiers were required to remain on campus except between 5 p.m. and 11 p.m. weekdays and between 3 p.m. Saturday and 6:15 a.m. Monday. They had to show a pass coming or going that was void beyond 50 miles of Tacoma.

Ah, but the weekends. Everyone looked forward to the weekends. A faculty War Activities Committee provided "entertainment, social functions, devotional services, and cultural programs for the uniformed men on our campus." This was nice. But the women on campus didn't need a committee to help them think of things to do. For example, in December our guy Cole was invited to an off-campus waffle breakfast. There he met freshman Alice Ann Cross. They hit it off, and Alice Ann invited Cole to be her date at the Feb. 1944 Tolo dance. After Cole's March 1944 departure, Alice Ann and Cole corresponded, and they kept it up throughout the war. Cole got out of the army in 1946, and after Alice Ann graduated they married, on June 14, 1947. Theirs is one of a few ASTP-related romances that led to marriage.

When their daughter, Liz Herdman, brought Cole to campus during Homecoming last October, they were greeted by Liz's son, Cole's grandson, Puget Sound freshman Cole Herdman '20. The family toured Kittredge Hall, all decked out for 75th-anniversary events, and found a brochure that they used as a historical guide through the building. On page 6 was a photograph of students seated on the lawn by the building's cornerstone. One of them was Alice Ann Cross. On another page they found dean of women Lyle Ford Drushel, who had attended Alice Ann and Cole's wedding. After that weekend Liz wrote to me, and on Dec. 28, 2016, I met in person Cole, Liz, and grandson Cole. This was a memorable moment for an old archives volunteer, witnessing the enthusiasm and interest that extended from Grandpa Cole, 18 years old in 1943, to grandson Cole, 18 years old now, in an important if brief era in Puget Sound history.

The ASTP sponsored a semiformal military ball on March 3, 1944. Cole was on the committee in charge of arrangements. By the time the 1944 *Tamanawas* was published, the soldiers had been gone for three months. Nevertheless, Puget Sound students devoted six yearbook pages to the ASTP. They wrote: "To the 238 members of the Army Specialized Training Unit, your staff members, and your officers, we dedicate this section with the hope that memories of your short stay with us will remain with you always."

They have, according to Cole Barnard, who still has his copy of that yearbook, along with memories of the girl he met and married.

Clinton Cole Barnard, ASTP Unit 3966 soldier, 1944. A version of this image appears on page 31 of the 1944 Tamanawas.

Lamp of learning and sword insignia of the ASTP.

Army Specialized Training Program

ASTP buddies C. Cole Barnard, left, and Edmund Buck outside the gymnasium, home of Company B, with Jones and Howarth halls in the distance, 1944.

Faces Behind the Buildings

Women students outside the south door of Kittredge Hall, 1944. Second from right is Alice Ann Cross '47, the future Mrs. Barnard.

Army Specialized Training Program

Alice Ann Cross '47 and C. Cole Barnard on their wedding day, June 14, 1947, at Christ Episcopal Church, Tacoma.

Faces Behind the Buildings

9. McIntyre Hall

When students arrived on campus to begin the school year in September 1964, they found a bright red truck sitting in the middle of Sutton Quadrangle with a drilling rig attached, pounding away. Some thought the college was drilling for oil to supplement its revenues. Actually a new building was to be built across the quadrangle from Howarth Hall, and the drilling had something to do with it. Oil was not the objective, though. Water was.

Everyone, including President Thompson, assumed the noise from the pile driver would be brief, as water was thought not to be too far down. But the drilling and the noise continued day after day. President Thompson may well have lost some of his hair over the well-drilling episode. "Haven't hit water yet—should we quit? No, we can't quit. We've come this far; surely we'll find water in another day or two." Meanwhile, students and faculty, while complaining, were becoming accustomed to the noise. Drilling continued throughout the entire fall semester and stopped when water was finally found at 917 feet, some 600 feet below sea level.

The water was for a heat pump for the building, to be named McIntyre Hall. The plan was to extract heat from 52-degree water and to return it at 34 degrees. Hilton Bowen Gardner Memorial Fountain is located over the deep shaft of the well dug on Sutton Quad.

McIntyre Hall is named for Charles Edwin McIntyre, who was a public relations officer for Weyerhaeuser and a strong supporter of the university. After his death, President Thompson discussed the need for a new building with Charles' daughter, Lucy McIntyre Jewett '50, who became a college trustee, and her husband, George F. Jewett, Jr. They supported the idea of a building in her father's memory and subsequently most of the $836,488 required to build McIntyre Hall was donated by Charles' descendants and by the George F. Jewett Foundation. Bids were opened in January 1965. Construction took place during the 1965–66 academic year. On May 23, 1966, Mrs. McIntyre cemented the cornerstone into place. The next day more than 1,000 people toured the new building, which housed the departments of economics and business administration (a combined program in those days), and sociology.

Vander Ende Forum, the large, tiered classroom on the west end of the first floor, was dedicated October 5, 1967, in memory of Gerrit P. Vander Ende, a businessman, Puget Sound trustee, and community leader. Wrote President Thompson of Vander Ende in 1978, "He proved to be one of the ablest trustees the university has had in many years." It was Vander Ende who, during the May 14, 1966, meeting of trustees, made the motions that New Hall be named for John D. Regester and that the new science building be named for R. Franklin Thompson.

Directly below Vander Ende Forum is Rausch Auditorium, named for Clarence George Rausch. His daughter, Susan, and her future husband, Peter Misner, both sang in the Adelphian Concert Choir as students. Together they later made it possible for Rausch Auditorium to be dedicated.

Battin Lounge was named for former debate coach and professor of economics Charles Thomas Battin, one of the most popular professors ever to teach at Puget Sound. Battin joined the faculty in 1926 and retired in 1955. During the war years 1943–45 he served as the National War Labor Board's wage stabilization director for Alaska.

An interesting feature of McIntyre Hall is the flat exterior roof on the west end. This was thought by President Thompson to be a nice location for an outdoor patio. The view from that location is indeed one of the loveliest on campus, although few have ever seen it.

Dean of faculty Robert Bock and President R. Franklin Thompson at the McIntyre Hall construction site, August 22, 1965.

Faces Behind the Buildings

In June 1969 students enjoy the coolness of the Hilton Bowen Gardner Memorial Fountain, built in 1967 atop the well that was dug on Sutton Quad for McIntyre Hall's heat pump.

McIntyre Hall

In 1964, drillers went down 600 feet below sea level before finding water for the McIntyre Hall heat pump—weird on a campus where, in other places, springs overflow on the surface.

McIntyre Hall, the third building on Sutton Quad, was built in one year. It opened in May 1966. We see it here in November 1966 during its first semester of use.

Faces Behind the Buildings

10. Memorial Fieldhouse
The Commencement Story

Memorial Fieldhouse, dedicated to the memory of Puget Sound students and Pierce County residents who lost their lives in World War II, opened in April 1949 and was thereafter the site for spring Commencement ceremonies through 1994. Beginning in spring 1995, Commencement was held outdoors on Peyton Field in Baker Stadium "rain or shine." Why no longer in Memorial Fieldhouse, protected from spring storms? Read on.

Early photographs show the field house as it was originally built, with a seating capacity of more than 6,000 and tall windows that allowed sunlight to stream through the south facing exterior wall. The central core was one big room. It was huge—the largest public venue in Pierce County—and was host to high school basketball tournaments, circuses, big-name musical performances and famous orators, and daffodil festivals. Then in 1983 the Tacoma Dome opened, and that changed everything for the field house and for the university.

As the need to maintain capacity for big public events disappeared—those events having moved to the dome—the university had much greater flexibility in configuring the field house to meet its changing needs. Modifications to the building over the years included interior walls on the south end of the great room to house a couple of classrooms, a dance studio, fitness facilities, an upstairs basketball court, and an exercise physiology lab. The tall windows disappeared.

Alas, as graduation class sizes increased in the 1980s, these modifications reduced occupancy to about 3,000. Eventually, seniors were issued seating tickets—four each. But the typical graduate wanted to invite 15 family and friends, not just four. An overflow video viewing site in Thompson Hall was unpopular, and a "black market" in Commencement seating tickets emerged. Commencement in Memorial Fieldhouse limped along through 1994, with the city's fire marshal watching closely to ensure safe capacity was not exceeded.

What to do? No one wanted to move the ceremony to the Tacoma Dome or anywhere else off campus. And memory of a cold and windy one-time late-1970s outdoor Commencement attempt had faded. In 1995 we tried it.

Good luck! The sun shined and the day was glorious. Outdoor Commencement was a resounding success. But what if it *had* rained? For the first few years outdoors, Memorial Fieldhouse was set up as a bad-weather backup site, with graduates continuing to receive four tickets, just in case. In poll after poll, though, year after year, seniors made it clear they would rather be outdoors in the rain with their grandparents, aunts, uncles, cousins, and friends, than dry indoors with just their parents and maybe a sibling or two. Eventually the Memorial Fieldhouse backup plan went away, and "outdoors rain or shine" became a Puget Sound tradition. It *does* rain sometimes, of course—the 1996 and 2011 classes got especially wet, and the 2014 ceremony!—we'll get to that in a moment. But most soaked graduates report that their shared Commencement experience promotes class identity.

May 2014 may have been a bit much, however. For the first time thunder and lightning in the area introduced an element of physical danger to the proceedings. Graduates hustled to the haven of Memorial Fieldhouse to wait out the storm before returning to Peyton Field to receive their diplomas, their lineup order still perfect. During their moments of exile Commencement speaker

Rachel Martin '96 delivered the Commencement address to family and friends under cover in Baker Stadium and to graduates watching on video screens in the field house. Sometimes, even with a "rain or shine" philosophy of which we are proud in Puget Sound's Pacific Northwest environs, compromise is required. And after 2014, Memorial Fieldhouse was once again set up as a planned backup site for Commencement.

The field house is still used for some public events, such as the March 2014 memorial service for former Washington Gov. Booth Gardner. That Memorial Fieldhouse no longer works well for Commencement seems a small price to pay for a building that has evolved from a large, almost single-purpose open space to a versatile structure that houses a great variety of student activities. And its evolution continues, with major renovations in 2015 and the attached Athletics and Aquatics Center that opened in fall 2016.

Faces Behind the Buildings

11. The Music Building

The physical address for the campus is generally given as 1500 N. Warner St., which is actually smack in the middle of the Jones Hall foyer. Were a physical address to be given to the Music Building, 1503 North Puget Sound would do. When Puget Sound moved from its Sixth and Sprague location to the current campus in 1924, it inherited an apple orchard and a wooden house at that address. The house is where the story of the Music Building begins.

According to Donald Raleigh '40, the house was built by his grandfather, Tacoma city engineer Norton Lonstreth Taylor, between September and December 1908. The design was from *Craftsman* magazine, edited by Gustav Stickley. Raleigh was born in the house in 1918.

College of Puget Sound President Edward Todd had to decide what to do with the house, located just west of Jones Hall. Most students commuted from their homes in those days but some were from out of the area, and the house became a dormitory for non-resident women.

Known as "Sacajawea Cottage," the first group of 16 students moved in for the 1924–25 academic year. Each year thereafter through 1929–30 the cottage housed between seven and 18 women and a house mother—Louisa Goulder through 1928–29 and Marie Tait during 1929–30. Marie made cakes for her charges on their birthdays.

After the 1929–30 school year, the cottage was remodeled yet again to become the Music Conservatory. The college's music program was housed there for more than two decades, but by 1950 the house was in bad shape and had become a fire hazard. President R. Franklin Thompson learned how shabby the building was when he leaned against a fireplace mantle and it fell to the floor in a cloud of soot.

The *Tacoma Daily Index* in early November 1950 printed an invitation to contractors to submit bids for construction of a new music building. Unfortunately the lowest bid was $75,000 more than the trustees expected to spend. The contractor who submitted the lowest bid agreed to wait 45 days while the trustees went to work finding additional money. This effort was unsuccessful and bids were solicited anew. The Strom Construction Company was selected as general contractor, and groundbreaking took place following the Commencement ceremony on Sunday, June 1, 1952. Sacajawea Cottage was dismantled board by board, since the new building was to occupy the same ground.

The Music Building opened for limited instruction in the summer of 1953 and was completed late that fall. More than 500 people attended an open house on Sunday, November 22, 1953. The new Music Building featured a record-listening room, a library for the department's collection of recorded and sheet music, 21 practice rooms with the capacity for 20 more, a student lounge, a faculty lounge, new sound and recording equipment, 30 new pianos, several performance and academic classrooms, and a 250-seat recital hall named posthumously in the 1960s for music Professor Leonard Jacobsen.

The Music Building is the only unnamed major building on campus. The person who was most in the running for the naming honor was Samuel Perkins, former owner of the *Tacoma Ledger* and *Daily News*. Perkins had given to the college before, including funds for the bust of Edward H. Todd that is on display today in Collins Memorial Library. Perkins pledged to give $150,000 toward the $425,000 cost of the music building. The trustees agreed that if he did so, the building would be named for him, but Perkins gave only $50,000 before his death. His estate, according to his children, could not produce the remaining $100,000. The Music Building was therefore not named Perkins Hall.

Another name deserves mention in connection with the Music Building, that of J. Bruce Rodgers. When Professor Rodgers joined the College of Puget Sound faculty as director of the Department of Music in September 1952, the new Music Building was only a hole in the ground. He therefore had time to tweak the plans to incorporate features that were important to the eventual successful use of the facility. For example, the door to the concert hall was made large enough to get a grand piano in. The band room was lowered so that the musicians on the rear tier of risers would not hit their heads on the ceiling.

The Music Building was the first classroom building to be constructed after Jones and Howarth halls were built in the 1920s. Music Building classrooms were used for English and history classes, as well as for music classes, until the music program grew to the point that it required all of the instructional space. Leonard Jacobsen Recital Hall was replaced by the much larger Schneebeck Concert Hall in 2002.

Faces Behind the Buildings

Professor of Music J. Bruce Rodgers accepts a shipment of pianos for the new Music Building, 1953.

House at 1503 North Puget Sound being remodeled and enlarged in 1924 to become "Sacajawea Cottage" women's dormitory, and later the Music Conservatory, located on the site of today's Music Building. The boardwalk led to Jones Hall.

The Music Building

Music Building under construction, 1953.

A very young Professor LeRoy Ostransky at work in the old Music Conservatory, 1948.

Faces Behind the Buildings

12. Puget Sound's Bells and Carillon

Bells of one kind or another have tolled on the Puget Sound campus since the 1930s. The vessel *Heather* carried the college's first bell across the waters of Commencement Bay from Browns Point on November 29, 1933. Cast in Pennsylvania in 1855, the bell served in stations on the Strait of Juan de Fuca and on Puget Sound until, with the automation of the Browns Point Lighthouse, President Edward Todd acquired the bell for the college. The bell was placed prominently in the Jones Hall first-floor foyer and was dedicated during Founders' and Patrons' Day celebrations on February 20, 1934. Speaking about the history of the bell on that occasion was longtime Browns Point Lighthouse keeper Oscar V. Brown.

After the excitement surrounding its arrival and dedication died down, the bell languished for some 13 years as a static object of admiration in Jones Hall, although it was sometimes struck for effect on special occasions. Then during the winter of 1947 "PLC [Pacific Lutheran College] students called attention to [the bell] by trying to steal it," according to *The Trail*. They failed because of the bell's 1,100-pound weight, but the next summer a heavy wooden gallows structure was built within which the bell was suspended outdoors. A mechanical mechanism was attached to regularize the bell's tolling and a bell house was constructed. Located along the wooden sidewalk between Jones Hall and the Music Conservatory, the bell house was, sometime during 1948, painted with graffiti alluding to its resemblance to an outhouse.

For a few short years the bell regularly pealed across campus from the bell house. But early in the 1950s, when water damaged the electrical mechanism and the bell cracked beyond repair, it was relegated to ignominious storage beneath the carpenters' shops in South Hall (razed in 2011). During the 1980s Puget Sound returned the old bell to Browns Point, where it resides today in Browns Point Lighthouse Park, watched over by the Points Northeast Historical Society.

In November 1954 Puget Sound acquired a magnificent set of bells, thanks to the generosity of trustee chair William W. Kilworth (for whom Kilworth Chapel is named), when he gave to the college the Howard R. Kilworth Memorial Carillon, in memory of his brother. The 61-bell Arlington model carillon was manufactured by Schulmerich Carillons Inc. of Sellersville, Pennsylvania. Still selling carillons today, the Schulmerich company remains proud that "founder George Schulmerich discovered that tiny rods of cast bronze struck with miniature hammers produced barely audible, but pure, bell tones and that these sounds could be amplified electronically to produce a rich, sonorous tone." Mr. Schulmerich called these small, cast bronze bells "carillonic bells," and these were the bells in the college's new carillon.

The "bells" and electronic mechanisms were housed in cabinets in an unfinished space at the north end of the third floor of the then-new Music Building. The electronically amplified "pure bell tones" were broadcast from special speakers (called horns) on the roof of Collins Memorial Library. The carillon chimed the hours and, in addition, was an instrument of the music faculty. Each Sunday at 2 p.m., music Professor John Cowell sat at the carillon's keyboard console in the music building and gave half-hour live concerts. The Sunday concerts continued well into the 1970s. The carillon also played pre-recorded music, much like a player piano, from the 150 plastic vinyl rolls in the music department's collection. The alma mater played every day.

At the November 12, 1954, dedication ceremony the carillon's keyboard console was moved to the Music Building's recital hall, where Princeton University bellmaster Arthur Lynde Bigelow played a live dedicatory concert. The concert began with Puget Sound's alma mater and ended with *Old Nassau*, Princeton's alma mater. George Schulmerich himself traveled from Pennsylvania for the carillon's installation and dedication.

While a marvel for its time, the carillon had mechanical properties that allowed it to be fiddled with. In 1975, Jeff Strong '76 figured out how to increase from 12 to 13 the number of times the bell tolled at noon. It was the perfect campus prank, as the carillon tolled 13 times every noon thereafter for several years.

Then, about 1979, the carillon fell abruptly silent, apparently unrepairable. No bells or chimes marked the passing of the hours and no joyous live concerts lifted campus spirits until in 1982 a newer generation Schulmerich carillon mechanism replaced the original. The 1982 carillon continued to use the bronze "carillonic bells" of the 1954 model, but the "instructions" to ring the bells came from digital tapes rather than the earlier mechanical mechanism. A new keyboard console replaced the original. Through the 1980s and 1990s, music Professor Edward Hansen performed occasional live concerts, including for the university's 1988 centennial.

After almost two decades of use, the 1982 carillon became unreliable and ceased operations for days at a time. In the fall of 2001 the college acquired a newer generation Schulmerich carillon, the Campanile Digital AutoBell Instrument. This carillon is what we hear today. It is essentially a computer and the bronze "carillonic bells" are no longer struck. Nevertheless, the ringing sounds like real bells and most people cannot tell the difference. Today's carillon resides in the upper reaches of Collins Memorial

Library, not in the Music Building. There is no longer a keyboard console for live concerts. The carillon rings the hours of the day and for many years played various tunes at noon and at 5 p.m. On May 9, 2016, the various tunes at noon were replaced by the daily playing of the alma mater, which had not been heard across campus for many years.

What about that other bell on campus, you ask, the one in Kilworth Chapel? It rings occasionally, for some services and weddings. Kilworth's bell is ancient. Made in 1718 in Sheffield, England, the bell has rung on ships and in churches and was used as a dinner bell by the Henry Vollmer family before the Vollmers gave it to Puget Sound.

A few months ago I teamed up with Jeff Strong—yes, *that* Jeff Strong, he of 13-chimes-at-noon fame. Jeff is now well into his fourth decade as a Puget Sound employee in the technology services department. When I showed him a 1954 photograph of George Schulmerich with the original carillon, Jeff said, "I think it might still be there—that old carillon—in the Music Building!" We had to go see. Jeff and I found archaeological gold in room 301, a large, secure janitor's closet. The five cabinets containing the original 61 bronze "carillonic bells" hang on the wall today as they have since 1954. The 1954-era mechanical control cabinets that Jeff reprogrammed in 1975 are gone, but the 1982 digital tape control cabinets remain, as does the keyboard console on which Edward Hansen played live concerts. All of this equipment is obsolete, unused, and dignified in dusty repose. That it is still there is to me amazing and fantastic. It's why I do this.

Puget Sound's Bells and Carillon

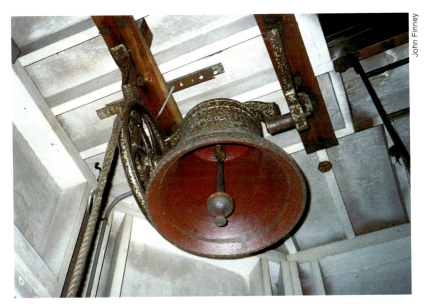

Seen here in 2004, this bell in the bell tower of Kilworth Chapel was cast in 1718 in Sheffield, England.

The bell house along the wooden walkway between Jones Hall and the Music Conservatory housed the campus bell between 1947 and 1953.

Faces Behind the Buildings

Arthur Lynde Bigelow, bellmaster of Princeton University, plays the dedicatory concert of the new Howard R. Kilworth Memorial Carillon, in the Music Building recital hall, November 12, 1954. The concert began with Puget Sound's alma mater and ended with Princeton's alma mater, "Old Nassau."

In November 1953 John Regester, dean of faculty and professor of philosophy, and J. Bruce Rodgers, professor of music, examine the campus bell, here lying in a corner of the carpenters' shop in South Hall (razed in 2011). The bell was cast in Pennsylvania in 1855 and warned ships of danger in the Strait of Juan de Fuca and in Puget Sound until 1934, when the college acquired it. Tamanawas, *1954.*

Puget Sound public relations director Robert E. Sconce, left, and George J. Schulmerich, of Schulmerich Carillons, Sellersville, Pennsylvania, with the just-installed 61-bell Schulmerich Arlington Carillon, on the top floor of the Music Building, November 12, 1954.

Faces Behind the Buildings

Jeff Strong '76 examines wiring diagrams of the 1954 and 1982 Schulmerich Arlington model campus carillons in the Music Building, January 19, 2016. The five boxes on the wall contain the 1954 carillon's "carillonic bells."

Puget Sound's current Schulmerich Carillon in the upper reaches of Collins Memorial Library, 2009.

Horns (loudspeakers) on the roof of Collins Memorial Library have projected the sounds of Puget Sound's carillons since 1954.

The five cabinets on the wall containing the 61 "carillonic bells" from 1954, the 1982 Schulmerich digital tape carillon, and the keyboard console for the 1982 carillon, January 19, 2016.

Faces Behind the Buildings

13. Regester Hall

John Dickinson Regester arrived at the College of Puget Sound as a 26-year-old professor of philosophy and psychology in the fall of 1924, the same semester Jones Hall opened on the new campus. Prior to coming to Puget Sound, Professor Regester served as a naval hospital corpsman with the Marines in France during World War I. He was a 1918 graduate of Allegheny College and later earned S.T.B. and Ph.D. degrees at Boston University. As a scholar, John Regester was known principally for his study of and his relationship with Albert Schweitzer, who referred to him as "my first American friend." His doctoral dissertation was titled "Immediate Intuition in a New Rationalism of Albert Schweitzer."

In 1924 philosophy and psychology were one academic department at the College of Puget Sound. Professor Regester taught all the college's philosophy courses, as well as some psychology courses. President Edward Todd had his eye on Professor Regester and in 1936 made him dean of the college. As John Regester's academic leadership abilities became increasingly evident, most of the daily administrative burden fell on his shoulders.

In addition to the academic operation of the college, Regester's responsibilities included the non-academic welfare and discipline of men, as was true of all deans in those days. Women students had been in the care of a dean of women at Puget Sound since 1922. When dean of men became a separate administrative position in 1948, Dean Regester's title was changed to dean of the faculty. (The title academic vice president for the top academic administrator came from the corporate world after Regester retired.) In 1960 Dean Regester became dean of the graduate school, as the university expanded degree offerings during R. Franklin Thompson's presidency.

Todd Hall was the college's first dormitory for men, opening in January 1948. A second men's residence hall was built in 1957. But because of unusually high enrollment of freshmen women, the new men's residence hall housed women during its first year of use, 1957–58, and was called Freshmen Hall. After Tenzler Hall (later known as University Hall, and currently known as Oppenheimer Hall) opened in fall 1958, the women of Freshmen Hall returned to "the women's side of campus." Regester thereafter housed men and was known as New Hall until May 14, 1966, when New Hall was renamed Regester Hall in honor of John D. Regester's 42 years of service to the college as professor, scholar, and dean. He remains Puget Sound's longest-serving academic dean. He was much loved, and the scope of his career and his influence contributed broadly to what we are today as a college. The 1950 *Tamanawas* is dedicated to him, and our memory of John Regester comes alive each November as a distinguished member of our faculty delivers the annual Regester Lecture.

During the 1964–65 academic year, my girlfriend and wife-to-be, Karen Peterson '67, P'94, and I were sophomores at Puget Sound. She was a resident of Harrington Hall; I of Regester when it was known as New Hall. Harrington, for women, and New Hall, for men, were built the same year to essentially the same architectural design, and residents of the two halls felt a kinship of sorts, or at least a competitive spirit.

The 1965 *Tamanawas* mentions "the annexation of Harrington Hall" by the men of New Hall. The following incident was not a part of the written record, until now. Late one Friday night the men of New Hall, with the complicity of some of the women of Harrington but not with the knowledge of Harrington's head resident, Alice Dodds, carried the furniture from the New Hall dorm room of Rich Crow '67 across campus to the front lounge of Harrington. There they recreated Rich's room. When Rich discovered his furniture was missing, his dormmates blindfolded him, led him across campus, and made him get into his own bed. When he took off his blindfold he was amazed to find himself in bed in a women's dorm, a situation he theretofore thought highly unlikely. About then Alice Dodds appeared and the furniture was quickly returned to New Hall, but the annexation legend was born.

New Hall (now Regester Hall) stands alone in 1963, before Seward and Phibbs Halls were built. The 1958 Chevy belonged to head residents Gordon and Linda Besel.

John Dickinson Regester was professor and dean at Puget Sound for 41 years, 1924–1965.

14. Seward Hall

Constructed in 1970, Seward Hall was dedicated in honor of Professor Emeritus Raymond Sanford Seward and Olive Brown Seward on July 27, 1972. The building is distinctive in at least three ways.

First, it is the only building named for someone who served his or her entire Puget Sound career on the faculty. (The building to which Seward Hall is attached by a portico, Regester Hall, is the only other building named for a professor. John Regester served on the faculty from 1924 to 1936 and as dean from 1936 to 1965.)

Second, Seward Hall is unique for being the only building named for a Puget Sound staff member. Olive Brown Seward served as presidential secretary for 27 years, first to Edward H. Todd and then to R. Franklin Thompson.

Finally, until 2013, Seward Hall was the only residence hall with five stories. The significant grade on which Seward Hall was built required a fifth floor to keep its roofline somewhat even with Regester Hall's. Thomas Hall (known as Commencement Hall until 2016) opened in fall 2013 as the second residence hall with five stories.

Both Raymond Seward and Olive Seward contributed significantly to Puget Sound. Raymond was born February 7, 1889, at Monticello, Iowa, one of four children born to Arthur and Sarah Seward. After teaching in high schools and a military academy in California, Raymond Seward joined the College of Puget Sound physics department in 1923 at age 34. He worked one year at the old Sixth and Sprague campus before the college moved to its current location. In addition to teaching, Professor Seward was "volunteered" for duty as the college's first track coach by a group of students who wanted to run and knew their physics prof had a track background. He also assisted with football coaching. In 1932 Professor Seward married President Todd's secretary, Olive Brown.

During his tenure at Puget Sound, Seward taught many brilliant students who went on to successful careers, including R. Ronald Rau '41 (now deceased), a former Puget Sound trustee, who served as senior physicist at the Brookhaven National Laboratory in New York.

Professor Seward retired in 1955 and became emeritus professor of physics. He died at age 89 on December 27, 1978.

Olive Brown was a College of Puget Sound student at the Sixth and Sprague campus and began service as President Todd's secretary in June 1919. President Todd considered her hiring to be an "important event," not only because of her longevity in the position, but for her good judgment. In his *History of the College of Puget Sound*, President Todd wrote that Olive Brown Seward was "faithful in the performance of her duties," was "well informed on the work of the college," and was someone faculty, students, and visitors could come to for information and get it. According to President Emeritus Todd's other book, *A Practical Mystic: Memoir of Edward Howard Todd*, Olive Brown Seward "became an encyclopedia of college lore" who "knew when and how to reveal her knowledge and was a good counselor, with the full confidence of the president." Olive Brown helped President Todd identify, purchase, and then move to the college's current campus in 1924. After President Todd retired in 1942, Olive Brown Seward served as President Thompson's secretary, until she retired in 1946.

The contributions of Raymond and Olive Seward to the college are the kinds of service it is not always possible to recognize when naming a building—teaching, influencing directly the lives of students, ensuring the smooth running of an administrative office, counseling decision-makers. These contributions are honored in Seward Hall.

Olive Brown Seward at her Jones Hall desk in the president's office.

Faces Behind the Buildings

Seward Hall, built in 1970, seen here in 1973.

Raymond Seward in Howarth Hall the year he retired from teaching, 1955.

15. South Hall

The 1947 *Tamanawas* contains an aerial view of campus that shows a field east of Warner Gym, newly cleared for the war-surplus buildings that would soon be erected there. In 1948 *Tamanawas* pictures the "new" buildings in place—South Hall.

In August 1946 Congress enacted the Mead Bill, authorizing the government to make available to colleges at no cost certain war-surplus buildings when the colleges could demonstrate that the buildings would be used to further the education of war veterans. President R. Franklin Thompson submitted the required application in February 1947. Documenting the need for additional space to serve the college's expanding enrollment of veterans was easy. In preparing the application, President Thompson and Alonzo Emerson, the college's then superintendent of buildings and grounds, made an extensive tour of the available war-surplus buildings in Washington and Oregon. The structures they deemed best for the college were the temporary hospital buildings TS-432, 433, and 434 at Paine Field Hospital in Everett, Washington. These buildings were finished on the inside, unlike all the others they looked at.

The college's bid for the buildings was approved by the War Emergency Housing Board, and at government expense they were moved to the campus in 18-by-25-foot sections and reassembled. The college paid to bring water and power to the site. South Hall was ready for use in late spring 1947. The easternmost building was, from the beginning, used by the buildings and grounds department, known today as facilities services. The other two wings contained offices and classrooms for the occupational therapy, philosophy, English, and history programs. As the occupational therapy program and, later, the physical therapy program, grew, they gradually consumed all of the space. A fourth war-surplus building was later obtained and situated behind the original three.

Although South Hall was considered temporary, President Thompson had been warned by other college presidents that interim facilities have a way of becoming permanent. The years rolled by, and the college added new siding and painted the buildings in an attempt to match as closely as possible the color of the campus' brick buildings. That this effort may not have been successful is suggested by the speed with which South Hall became known as "the pink building." But South Hall was situated apart from the college's structural core, so that, according to President Thompson, it did "not necessarily hamper the total beauty of the basic campus." This did not prevent occupational therapy and physical therapy graduates from making known their desire for a new building when, each spring during Commencement, they handed President Phibbs and, later, President Pierce, pink-colored reminders, such as balloons, in exchange for their diplomas.

Their efforts seem to have paid off. In 2009 facilities services moved from South Hall to new space south of the field house. In 2011 occupational therapy and physical therapy moved from South Hall to Weyerhaeuser Hall, the new center for health sciences. After 64 years as a "temporary" facility, South Hall was then razed in one day. With South Hall out of the way, and with a new academic building located on North 11th Street across from Memorial Fieldhouse, the "basic campus" enlarged significantly, tied together from one end to the other by the new Commencement Walk.

South Hall

South Hall and Warner Gym as seen from a window on the south side of Todd Hall, 1949. (The scene from this perspective today is quite different: South Hall—gone, Hugh Wallace Memorial Pool—gone, North 13th Street—gone, Warner Street—gone, as the campus expanded southward.)

Faces Behind the Buildings

16. Thompson Hall

Thompson Hall was Puget Sound's second science building. The first was Howarth Hall, which housed science instruction for 44 years, between 1924 and 1968. A third science building, Harned Hall, was dedicated in 2007. A major renovation to Thompson Hall was completed in 2008, and Thompson became, with Harned to which it is connected, today's state-of-the-art science center. But for the 39-year period from 1968 to 2007, Thompson Hall stood alone as the university's science building.

With the surge of interest in science that occurred in the late 1950s and early 1960s, it became clear that Howarth Hall was inadequate to meet the instructional and research needs of the science curriculum. In 1960 President R. Franklin Thompson began working with chemistry Professor Robert Sprenger, biology Professor Gordon Alcorn, and physics Professor Martin Nelson on plans for an expanded science facility.

Their efforts occurred at the height of the Cold War. Congress had allocated $700 million for civil defense, some $425 million of which was to go for the construction of civil defense shelters across the country. The director of civil defense for the state of Washington felt that the University of Puget Sound was the ideal location for meeting the civil defense shelter needs of North Tacoma. This thinking merged with on-campus planning for a new science facility. The question planners addressed was, could the new facility be designed to fulfill the specifications for a civil defense shelter, thereby making the university eligible for government funds to aid in construction?

Because Howarth Hall was the existing science facility, the original thinking was that an additional science building should be constructed across Sutton Quadrangle from Howarth Hall, where McIntyre Hall now stands. Together, this new building and Howarth Hall would comprise the new science facility. To that notion was added the proposal that the area's civil defense needs could be met by underground science laboratories beneath Sutton Quadrangle. Covered with four feet of reinforced concrete and four feet of earth, the underground spaces could serve as shelter space and would provide below-ground physical connections between the old and the new science buildings. If the federal government's Office of Civil and Defense Mobilization accepted the plans, it would pay for 50 percent of the cost of construction.

As the deadline for application for civil defense construction money neared, President Thompson met in his office with science faculty for a final review of the plans they had been working on. At this early Monday morning meeting, the five chairs of the science departments and mathematics, along with President Thompson, came reluctantly to the same conclusion: The plan was unworkable and was too expensive in the long term. Problems included the venting of gases and fumes and the need to pump waste 40 feet uphill to access the sewer system.

The plan was abandoned. Also abandoned was the working assumption that the new science building should be located across from Howarth Hall. The planners' eyes turned westward, toward Union Avenue. Union had always been at the college's "back door," with Jones Hall looking down its "front door," North 15th Street. With the construction of Interstate 5, Union Avenue became a major new route for people driving to the university. Administrators and faculty began to realize that the university could have two "front doors."

The new science building was therefore designed as a three-winged facility on Union Avenue with its center facing North 15th Street to the west, just as Jones Hall centers on North 15th Street facing east. Groundbreaking for construction of the new 114,000-square-foot science building occurred on November 29, 1966. Classes were first held in the building January 3, 1968. The building and its contents cost approximately $4 million.

In a February 11, 1966, *Trail* editorial, Dennis Hale '66 proposed that the new science building be named for President Thompson, in recognition of his years of service to the college. The suggestion enjoyed broad support, and on May 14, 1966, the trustees made it official. When Thompson, or "Doc T" as he was affectionately known, became Puget Sound's 10th president in 1942, he was 34 years old, the youngest college president in the country. When Doc T retired in 1973, he was the longest-serving living U.S. college president. During his 31-year presidency, R. Franklin Thompson built, on average, one new building each year—of which Thompson Hall was one, increasing the number of permanent buildings on campus from four to 37.

Doc T is remembered for his fundraising abilities and for the buildings he added to the campus, but even more for his love for students and the college. He was a father figure to many who relied on him for support and advice. I remember Doc T speaking to students at various banquets in the Great Hall (now called Marshall Hall) of the student center. On one occasion just before winter break, Doc T urged us when we went home for the holidays to sit down with our parents to tell them how much we loved them and how much we appreciated what they did for us. And we did.

After retiring as president in 1973, Doc T was named by trustees as honorary chancellor for life. He maintained an office in Collins Memorial Library for two or three years before moving downtown, to 1 Washington Plaza. During the six years before he finally retired for good in 1979, Thompson aided fundraising efforts and wrote about the buildings, people, and events of his presidency. R. Franklin Thompson was 90 years old when he died on January 15, 1999. He was the last ordained Methodist minister among Puget Sound's 14 presidents.

Although Thompson Hall is today a much better facility than it was before it joined Harned Hall to become one of the best science complexes in the country, Thompson Hall is unique among the major campus buildings in the degree to which its architectural presence has been altered from its original grandeur. As an independent architectural presence Thompson Hall is essentially gone. Yet without question Doc T would have supported the decision that put the building named after him in Harned Hall's "backyard." For him the needs of the college always came first.

Professors Edward Goman, Gordon Alcorn, Robert Sprenger, and Martin Nelson view Thompson Hall construction, 1967.

Aerial view of Thompson Hall construction, 1967.

President R. Franklin Thompson at Thompson Hall construction site, 1967.

Faces Behind the Buildings

Aerial view of Thompson Hall, circa 1970.

President R. Franklin Thompson outside Thompson Hall, 1972.

17. Todd Hall

With the end of World War II and the passage of the GI Bill, enrollment of men at the College of Puget Sound increased dramatically. Anderson Hall for women had opened in 1939, but there was no permanent residence hall for men. Some men did live for a short time in South Hall, the "temporary" set of wooden buildings acquired as war surplus located east of Warner Gym. But President R. Franklin Thompson felt that new permanent student housing was needed for the college to become more residential as it moved away from its reputation as a commuter college, a niche he knew the two-year junior colleges would increasingly fill.

On July 15, 1946, ground was broken for Todd Hall. The shovel used at the groundbreaking was the same shovel used to break ground in 1938 for Anderson Hall. According to former President Edward H. Todd in his biography *A Practical Mystic*, for years the shovel was "labeled and preserved as a souvenir of the beginning of dormitory life on the campus."

Because building materials were hard to come by after the war, some 18 months were spent in the building of Todd Hall. The contract with Mr. L.B. McDonald was unusual, in that McDonald's responsibility was limited to the building's construction. The college itself purchased all of the building materials.

On June 14, 1947, with construction still in progress, a cornerstone-laying ceremony was held as part of the annual meeting on the campus of the Pacific Northwest Conference of the Methodist Church. The first men moved into Todd Hall in January 1948.

Todd Hall was named for Edward Howard Todd, president from 1913 to 1942. He was the man who helped the college find itself after the first turbulent 25 years.

Edward Todd himself troweled the Todd Hall cornerstone into place that June 14, 1947, day at age 84. He had earlier told President Thompson that, although he was known mostly for having been a fundraiser and the man who put the college on a firm financial footing, he was equally proud of the academic stature of the college and had always hoped to have his name on an academic building. But when the time came to build the first men's residence hall, he said he was proud it was to be named for him.

President Todd was responsible for the College of Puget Sound's move to its current location in 1924, and was responsible for the architectural style of the campus. Twenty-three years later he was reported to have said that "the present location was decided on the basis that the city of Tacoma would never reach out far enough to surround the school." It did, of course.

Edward Todd was born in Council Bluffs, Iowa, on April 2, 1863. When he became president he was 50 years old. He retired from the presidency and became president emeritus on July 31, 1942, at age 79. He turned the college over to a much younger man, also from Willamette, R. Franklin Thompson, age 34, who served as president for 31 years. The new President Thompson asked former President Todd if he would write a history of the college. Working throughout the 1940s in an office in the basement of Jones Hall, Todd wrote not only the history, but his memoirs as well. On December 15, 1947, Todd completed the history and on the same day celebrated the 60th anniversary of his marriage to Florence Anne Todd.

When we consider the heroes of the college, Edward Howard Todd is in the first rank. Just as President Ronald Thomas and others are the heroes of the current era in the life of our college, Edward Todd fought—and won—the early battles that had to be waged for Puget Sound to survive and prosper. He is in that sense much with us still. As we pass by the cornerstone near the northeast door of Todd Hall, let us think of the man who laid the foundation of the college we know and love today. We owe much to Todd, whose story is told in greater depth elsewhere in this volume.

Just as in 1954 Anderson Hall was joined with Langdon Hall to become Anderson-Langdon, so in 1990 Todd Hall was joined with Phibbs Hall to become Todd-Phibbs.

Former President Edward H. Todd, second from right, turns a shovelful of dirt at the Todd Hall groundbreaking ceremony on July 15, 1946. Others in the photograph are, from left: President R. Franklin Thompson, trustee chair William W. Kilworth, and ASCPS President Philip Garland.

Todd Hall, the second residence hall (after Anderson Hall), stands alone on the quadrangle in 1952, before the construction of Regester or Trimble halls. South Hall (razed in 2011) is visible at left.

18. Warner Gymnasium

Warner Gym was completed in 1924, along with Jones Hall and the basement of the science building, later known as Howarth Hall. Together, the three structures comprised the "new campus" after the college moved from its Sixth and Sprague site. While Jones and Howarth are constructed of bricks and masonry, Warner Gym is a wood-framed building with a brick veneer. According to Edward H. Todd, college president 1913–42, some of the wood material used in construction of the gymnasium was salvaged from the Sixth and Sprague campus buildings.

For a quarter century Warner Gym was adequate for the athletic needs of the campus, but with the post-war growth in the student population the gym rocked and rolled in an increasingly cramped manner during basketball games. After Memorial Fieldhouse opened in April 1949, the old gym became known first as the Girls' Gym or the Women's Gym, and later as Warner Gym for its location on what would be Warner Street if Warner Street ran through the campus.

At the same time the gymnasium was built, a 10-acre athletic field was graded south and west of the gym. A May 17, 1924, photograph shows the athletic field being graded by genuine horsepower. Together, the new gymnasium and athletic field were designated the Athletic Quadrangle, one of 10 quadrangles envisioned for the new campus by architect Albert Sutton and President Todd.

This description of Warner Gym appeared in the four-page quarterly *College of Puget Sound Bulletin* for July 1924: "A new gymnasium 70 x 110 feet is under construction on North 13th

Street, south of C.H. Jones Hall. It is to have a maple basketball floor; and a good supply of showers and dressing rooms in the basement, which will have a cement floor. The north end—the front of the gym—will have offices on the ground floor; study rooms on the second and dormitories for men on the third floor. It will have a hot water heating plant."

The basketball court itself is on the second floor, extending to the height of the third floor. Originally, the basketball area's third-floor level contained windows to let in natural light. Some of the windows were later bricked over, diminishing the architectural symmetry and beauty of the building. Warner Gym was renovated to accommodate Hugh Wallace Memorial Pool, which opened in 1957 and was attached to the south end of the gym. In 2016 the pool was replaced by the new Athletics and Aquatics Center attached to Memorial Fieldhouse.

On Wednesday, March 12, 1947, coal in the gym's boiler room caught fire. The fire was doused by firemen to the cheers of students released from their afternoon classes for the occasion. Fortunately, the college had only the week before added some $100,000 to its campus insurance policy, which, according to bursar Gerard Banks, was adequate to repair the water-soaked, smoke-stained gym. The gym floor was refinished for the 1947–48 basketball season with a material called "Lastincote," made by the West Disinfectant Company.

Warner Gymnasium

Jones Hall and the under-construction gymnasium are the only buildings on campus in this view across the athletic field toward the northeast, September 1924.

The just-completed gymnasium, 1925.

Faces Behind the Buildings

1942 men's freshman basketball team in Warner Gymnasium.

Gymnasium floor refinished with "Lastincote," made by the West Disinfecting Company, October 1947. The new floor was made necessary by smoke and water damage from a March 1947 fire in the boiler room. This view shows the windows on the south exterior wall that were bricked over for construction of Hugh Wallace Memorial Pool.

Warner Gymnasium

Beloved coach and later Athletics Director John Heinrick dribbles the ball in Warner Gym, 1948.

People of Puget Sound

People of Puget Sound

19. Homer Amundsen and Boxing at Puget Sound

During the first half of the 20th century the three primary sports in America were baseball, horse racing, and boxing. Boxing was especially popular. During World War II boxing training was required of undergraduate men at Harvard to promote physical fitness and war readiness. By midcentury, television was a growing medium, and boxing matches were among the most-watched sporting broadcasts.

Feeding boxing's popularity at the collegiate level were World War II veterans who lobbied for boxing to be added to the athletic roster of sports.

Even the College of Puget Sound hopped onto the boxing bandwagon, briefly. In September 1950 the college announced that boxing would become a varsity sport, and that Homer Amundsen would coach the team. Amundsen was well known in Tacoma for the boxing gym he operated at 719 ½ Commerce St., and for the coaching work he did at the Starlight Athletic Club at South 11th and Market streets.

Amundsen set up a training room on the third floor of Warner Gymnasium featuring "a full-sized ring, punching bags, mirrors, exercise equipment, and autographed pictures on the walls."

During fall semester 1950 Coach Amundsen tried to assemble a team of student fighters for intercollegiate competition. About a dozen students tried out, but only four or five were truly competitive. Most had never boxed before. This was a problem, because Coach Amundsen needed eight fighters to fill out the team.

The most talented of Amundsen's boxers was undoubtedly three-time Golden Gloves winner, "Irish" Pat McMurtry. McMurtry transferred to Puget Sound from Gonzaga and enrolled for a full load of classes, including PE 59, Boxing.

Coach Amundsen faced another problem as well. No other college in the region had an intercollegiate boxing program. Eastern Washington State College had disbanded its boxing team the year before, reducing the pool of potential opponent schools from one to zero.

Coach Amundsen put on two exhibition matches in Memorial Fieldhouse, on November 20 and December 13. To cobble together an eight-man team Amundsen borrowed two Lincoln High School students and two additional non-CPS Tacomans to complement four of his Loggers. Their opponents were Seattle's Greenwood Boys Club and the Bremerton Athletic Club.

In January 1951, Director of Athletics John Heinrick announced that the effort to field an intercollegiate varsity boxing team was over, but that boxing would continue as an intramural sport. He said that, because the college could not field a team without bringing in outside fighters, Puget Sound would have had to acquire "an expensive" license from the state boxing commission, which the school elected not to pursue. He also mentioned what was perhaps the more serious problem, the absence of other colleges to box against.

Intramural boxing continued for a while, but before long the serious fighters, including McMurtry, withdrew from their spring classes and Coach Amundsen left the campus.

Although Pat McMurtry's connection with Puget Sound was brief, he was Amundsen's star pupil and went on to a successful career as a heavyweight fighter. Bill Baarsma '64, P'93 (author of "Field Goals" in the winter 2013 *Arches*) remembers watching McMurtry fight at Lincoln Bowl and claims him as one of his heroes growing up. McMurtry passed away at age 79 on April 17, 2011.

Through the 1950s college boxing declined in popularity. The National Collegiate Athletic Association (NCAA) first sanctioned boxing in 1937, but NCAA sponsorship of intercollegiate boxing team competition ended after 1960. In that year a University of Wisconsin boxer collapsed and died of a brain hemorrhage. But a few schools continued to sponsor boxing, and in 1976 the National Collegiate Boxing Association (NCBA) was established. Currently about 35 colleges participate in NCBA-sponsored events.

Logger boxing Coach Homer Amundsen with his team in Warner Gym training room, October 1950. From left: Virgil Larson, Lee Stahle, Terry McLean M.A. '58, Gary Featherstone, Pat McMurtry, and Amundsen.

People of Puget Sound

Homer Amundsen with his star boxer, "Irish" Pat McMurtry, 1950.

Gary Featherstone and "Irish" Pat McMurtry work out in Warner Gym, 1951.

"Irish" Pat McMurtry and Gary Featherstone.

People of Puget Sound

20. Coolidge Otis Chapman

Beginning in the early 1980s, students who have completed requirements of the Honors Program graduate as Coolidge Otis Chapman Honors Scholars. But who, exactly, was Coolidge Otis Chapman? And why are Honors Program graduates called Chapman scholars?

Coolidge Otis Chapman was born in New York in 1895, married in 1926, joined Puget Sound's English department in 1932, retired in 1959, and died in Tacoma in 1966. He was tall (6 feet 3 inches—always in the back row in photographs) and an extremely slender 150 pounds.

He did not come from humble beginnings. Coolidge was the oldest of three sons; his father was a successful architect and builder living in Woodmere, Hempstead Township, Nassau County, Long Island, New York.

All three boys were shipped off to Hoosac School, an Episcopal boarding school in Hoosick Falls, New York. After graduating from Hoosac, Coolidge enrolled at Williams College but transferred before graduating from Cornell University. At Cornell he earned bachelor's, master's, and Ph.D. degrees. His 1925 master's thesis, *The Diction of the Middle English Purity*, was the beginning of Coolidge's lifelong research interest. He spent several summers and his 1949–1950 and 1955–1956 sabbaticals at his alma mater, where he pursued research on the Pearl Poet, author of *Sir Gawain and the Green Knight*, considered to be "one of the four great writers of Medieval England." In 1951 Cornell University Press published Chapman's book, *An Index of Names in Pearl, Purity, Patience and Gawain*, "from poems of the late 14th century," according to the November 1, 1951, issue of *The Trail*. The book includes some 250 names "from the Bible, from the classics, and from Medieval romances." Since 1951 the book has gone through several editions.

But we are getting ahead of ourselves.

In 1926 Coolidge married Helen Hume; he was 31, she 30. Two years later the pair traveled from New York to Europe, arriving July 8 at Plymouth, England, on Holland America's *Rotterdam*. They returned from France three months later on the *Rijndam*, then moved to Williamstown, Massachusetts, where Coolidge began a four-year teaching stint at Williams College. In 1932 the pair came to Tacoma. They had two children, John and Helen. Coolidge's College of Puget Sound salary in 1940 was $2,600.

At the College of Puget Sound, Coolidge Otis Chapman found what he was looking for—a physical and intellectual home. He teamed up with Julius Peter Jaeger to form a dynamic duo that towered over the English department for decades and epitomized across the campus intellectual standing in teaching and rigor in research. Jaeger, who himself came to Puget Sound in 1929, was chair of the department until he retired in 1952. Chapman took over the chair position in 1952 for the last seven years of his Puget Sound career. Jaeger and Chapman were the only full professors in the English department for more than 30 years, until Harold Simonson attained that rank in the 1960s.

As soon as Chapman arrived at Puget Sound, he and Jaeger restructured the English department's literary studies curriculum. "Introduction to English Literature" and "World Literature," both yearlong courses, were required of all majors. Majors then selected upper-level literature courses from two groups. Group I—Professor Chapman's bailiwick—included medieval literature, Renaissance literature, and Shakespeare courses. Group II—Professor Jaeger's area—consisted of 18th- and 19th-century literature courses. Both profs had on occasion taught pretty much everything in the department, including required composition courses, but their basic teaching and literary research interests complemented each other perfectly and made for a smooth-running department. The two-group classification of upper-level literature courses continued in the English department from the early 1930s until after 1959.

Here is the description of a typical Coolidge Otis Chapman upper division course, the yearlong Old and Middle English Literature: "First semester: reading in selected translations from Old English prose and poetry, and in Middle English other than Chaucer. Second semester: rapid reading of Chaucer in the original. Discussion and reports." Old and Middle English Literature alternated every two years with Chapman's yearlong Literature of the English Renaissance.

When interviewed in 1947 by a *Trail* reporter, Professor Chapman named Dante, Chaucer, and Wordsworth as his favorite poets. But, he said, "Each is so great in his own way, that I cannot say which of them I admire most." Professor Chapman went on, "The purpose of literary studies is not merely to learn the names, dates, and works of the principal writers, but to build a philosophy of life by which one can live." Apparently Professor Chapman was good at transferring this enthusiasm to his students. The *Trail* reporter wrote: "Professor Chapman is so deeply interested in his profession that his classes vibrate under his interesting lectures. Dr. Chapman is regarded by all who know him as one of the most understanding and kindest professors at CPS."

Chapman retired from teaching at the end of the spring 1959 semester. A banquet attended by colleagues and students was held in his honor at the Top of the Ocean Restaurant. President R. Franklin Thompson presented Chapman with an inscribed silver tray, and Dean John Regester spoke of Professor Chapman's humility. In response to the accolades bestowed upon him, Professor Chapman said, "I think some of the things they said about me were pretty much exaggerated." Humility indeed.

In writing about the history of our college, we sometimes emphasize too much its buildings and administrative leaders. Development of the college to its current level of distinction is perhaps best understood through the increasing quality of the faculty. Certainly it never has been better. But one of the greats of the past who could be slipped into the current professorial milieu and counted among the best is Coolidge Otis Chapman. His approach to teaching was thoroughly modern. He declared that every class meeting was a new experience. "The students make them interesting. Each student brings a new mind, and I learn as much from them as they do from me—maybe a little more."

Professor Chapman enjoyed seven years of retirement before passing away of cancer at age 71 on August 29, 1966. Twelve years later, someone who knew Chapman well became director of a reinvigorated Honors Program, designed to be integrated with the new core curriculum. Professor Robert Albertson '44 was instrumental in helping to shape the form of the Honors Program, which continues essentially unchanged in its purpose to the present day. Since its implementation in 1979–1980, the Honors Program has promised that those who complete requirements of the program, including the critically important honors thesis, will be designated Coolidge Otis Chapman Honors Scholars at graduation, with that designation appearing on the academic transcript. The legacy of a tall, thin professor of literary studies lives on. Believing, as he said, that purposeful literary study can help "build a philosophy of life by which one can live," Professor Chapman continues to inspire students today.

Coolidge Otis Chapman

Some of the faculty teaching at the College of Puget Sound during the 1932–33 year. The tallest man in the back row is Professor Coolidge Otis Chapman. This was his first year at CPS. Tamanawas, 1933.

Left to right: A. D. Rugh, A. M.; C. O. Chapman, Ph. D., Christian Miller, A. M.; J. P. Jaeger, Ph. D.; Mrs. C. A. Robbins, Ph. MB.; W. E. Tomlinson, Ph. D.; Mrs. Lyle F. Drushel, A. M.; Miss Dorothy Punderson, A. M. Miss Linda Van Norden, A. M., C. A. Robbins, A. B., not in picture.

LANGUAGE AND LITERATURE

Language and literature faculty teaching at the College of Puget Sound during the 1937–38 year. While Coolidge Otis Chapman was a tall man and towered over others when standing, he tended to slouch when sitting, as demonstrated in this image. That's Chapman second from left. This was his sixth year at CPS. Tamanawas, 1938.

113

Cooledge Otis Chapman, Ph.D.

Professor of English Coolidge Otis Chapman. The arm and the hand on his shoulder belong to Chapman's English department colleague, Julius Peter Jaeger. Tamanawas, *1946.*

Professor Chapman stands inside Jones Hall with two unidentified students, 1948. The image is printed on page 23 of the 1948 Tamanawas *with this caption: "Student-faculty cooperation–part of the spirit of the College of Puget Sound."*

Professor Chapman in class, Jones Hall, 1951. The image is printed on page 86 of the 1951 Tamanawas *with the caption: "Dr. Chapman's class discussed world literature during the Renaissance."*

Faculty reception in Anderson Hall, September 1953. The men at right are Professor Chapman and biology Professor Gordon Alcorn. Note how Chapman at 6 feet 3 inches towers over the reasonably-tall-himself Gordon Alcorn. (The woman seated is Leone Murray, incoming dean of women, who replaced the retiring Lyle Ford Drushel, who served as dean of women between 1931 and 1953.)

People of Puget Sound

Professor Chapman waits for a bus in the CPS bus shelter, 1949. Again we see evidence that when the very tall Professor Chapman is not standing, he tends to slouch a bit. This image is printed on page 39 of the 1949 Tamanawas *with the caption "My lazy day."*

The dynamic duo of the English department for three decades, English professors Coolidge Otis Chapman, seated, and Julius Peter Jaeger, Jones Hall, circa 1950.

21. Edward H. Todd
The Man Who Saved Puget Sound

In 2013 we celebrated the 125th anniversary of the University of Puget Sound. But it might have been otherwise. We might instead have read in the "Looking Back 100 Years" section of the local newspaper that in 1913 the University of Puget Sound closed its doors for good after a valiant 25-year struggle. Puget Sound University, established by the Methodist Episcopal Church in 1888, was from the beginning subject to "an extraordinary succession of misfortunes," as former President Edwin Randall (1903–04) wrote in the 1930s. A large, elegant building was erected downtown, and classes began in 1890. The 1893 recession—almost a depression—was especially severe in the Pacific Northwest and had a devastating impact on the fledgling university's ability to raise or borrow money. In 1891 the school leased and then sold its new building to pay the construction debt, and had to rent less desirable facilities. A new vision opened up when land west of Tacoma became available. In 1894 the trustees created the University Land Company to sell lots around what they hoped would become the new campus in the suburb that came to be called University Place. More than 1,000 lots were sold, but the commissions paid to land company agents were so high that little money came into the trust fund set up to build a campus there. To meet operational expenses, the school's officers borrowed money from the trust fund, something that was not strictly legal. The financial house of cards finally collapsed in 1903, bringing Puget Sound University to a corporate end.

Its successor, the University of Puget Sound, was created in 1903 by the same conference of the Methodist Church that had given birth to Puget Sound University 15 years earlier. Optimism was high for the reborn institution. The college moved to a new location at Sixth and Sprague avenues and for the first time had a real—although small—campus. The Methodist churches of the conference pledged to contribute 50 cents per member each year in support of the college. But financial struggles continued with another economic recession in 1907. The college ended the 1912–13 academic year with revenues and operational expenses in balance, but without funds to make any headway on repayment of its $45,788 debt.

In September 1913 the annual conference of the Methodist Church debated a motion to close the school. It was a near thing. There were strong arguments on both sides. That the assembly declined to close the college did not much help the school's trustees solve their financial problems. President Julius Zeller (1909–13) was well regarded but had earlier tendered his resignation in light of the university's indebtedness. The day after the Methodist conference ended, the college's trustees directed their chair, Edward Blaine, to "*send for Todd!*"

But who was this Edward Howard Todd? Trustees and church leaders knew him well. An ordained Methodist minister, Todd had begun his affiliation with Puget Sound University in late 1897, when, at age 35, he joined the board of trustees. In 1905 he became the school's corresponding secretary, a financial officer who worked with the president to secure funds for the college. Todd was good at his job, but he had no control over the spending of the money. In 1909 Todd left Puget Sound, dismayed at the way money was borrowed and spent with no systematic plan for its repayment.

In 1913, when the financial crisis led to the proposal to close the school, Todd was serving as vice president of Willamette

University, the other Methodist college in the Pacific Northwest. Fifty years old and highly regarded, Todd was at the time mulling over with some enthusiasm the possibility he might be selected to open a new school of theology in the region. Edward Blaine's letter offering him the presidency of the University of Puget Sound was unexpected and not particularly welcome. Todd's experience with the school's financial situation gave him little hope for the future of the college.

But Edward Blaine and Everell Collins, longtime servants of the University of Puget Sound and heroes of the college in their own right, were persuasive. Finally, after many sleepless nights and prayers, Todd traveled to Tacoma with four "propositions" that he required the trustees to support before he would accept the presidency. One of the propositions was that the college would do only what it could afford to do. "We will do good work and pay for it," said Todd. The trustees agreed to the four propositions. Convinced of their full support, Edward Todd blazed with a renewed commitment to what the college could become. His acceptance of the presidency was, he wrote, "a contract with God."

Todd put the college's financial house in order, in the process achieving a goal previously thought to be unattainable: He met the $250,000 Hill Challenge. James J. Hill of St. Paul, Minnesota, the builder of the Great Northern Railway, the "empire builder" for whom our Seattle-to-Chicago long-distance passenger train is still named, had earlier agreed to give the college $50,000 if it raised $200,000. This was when most of the school's donors were poor church congregations scattered across a sparsely populated region. But Todd did it by the October 15, 1915, deadline.

Looking forward to a move to a new campus, the college in 1919 began a campaign to raise $1 million for buildings and endowment. The first half-million was to be raised from the citizens of Tacoma and Pierce County. A group of businessmen Todd called together to discuss the campaign said it couldn't be done. The second half-million was to be raised from the Methodist churches and their members in the conference. When, in 1921, the full million had been secured, trustees chair Edward Blaine wrote, "You have heard of the man who tackled the job which 'couldn't be done' and did it. His name is E.H. Todd. In fact, if any of you have a piece of work you wish left undone, pray don't place Dr. Todd in charge and tell him 'it can't be done.'"

Edward Todd worked hard and skillfully for the college for a very long time. He had to. When he became president in 1913, Todd's successor was only 5 years old, a little kid named Franklin, running around Primrose, Nebraska. If Todd knew in 1913 that he would have to persevere in the job until R. Franklin Thompson grew up, perhaps he would have had second thoughts. Instead his passion for Puget Sound kept him busy for 29 years. In 1924 Todd moved the school to its current campus and built Jones and Howarth halls and Warner Gymnasium, and established the architectural style of the campus. In 1939 he built Anderson Hall, the college's first permanent residence hall. And Kittredge Hall, the first student center, opened in 1942, the same year Todd retired at age 79.

For nine years, until his death in 1951, Todd remained an active member of the Puget Sound community. R. Franklin Thompson, only 34 years old when he succeeded Todd as president, valued Todd's mentorship and gave him an office in the basement of Jones Hall, where Todd wrote his memoir and a history of the college.

During its first 128 years, Puget Sound was served by 13 presidents—eight of them during the difficult first 25 years. Five presided during the next 103 years. Edward Todd was the first in

Puget Sound's string of strong, long-tenured leaders. R. Franklin Thompson served for 31 years. He had to. His successor, a kid named Phil, was only 10 when Thompson became president.

Edward H. Todd, R. Franklin Thompson, Philip M. Phibbs, Susan R. Pierce, and Ronald R. Thomas were strong leaders who led with the same fervor that energized Todd when he took over in 1913. Each made his or her distinctive mark on the college and advanced and improved it tremendously. But if in 1913 Edward Todd had not been sent for, we most likely would not today have our beloved college at all.

President Edward Howard Todd in his new Jones Hall office with portraits of Charles Hebard Jones and Franke Toby Jones, circa 1924. Franke Toby Jones gave $200,000 for construction of Jones Hall in memory of her husband Charles, who died in 1922, two years before Jones Hall opened.

President Edward Howard Todd, circa 1905. Todd seems stern in photographs, but he was highly regarded and respected throughout his long career as clergyman, traveling secretary, college vice president, and college president.

President R. Franklin Thompson, President Emeritus Edward H. Todd, and Tacoma businessman Samual A. Perkins with the bust of Edward Todd that today resides in Collins Memorial Library, January 1950. The bust, sculpted by Puget Sound art faculty member Kenn Glenn, was a gift to the college from Mr. Perkins.

22. Charles Arthur Robbins

Edward H. Todd, Puget Sound's president between 1913 and 1942, is generally considered to be the person who saved the college after its first 25 years of precarious existence. By dint of his fundraising and management skills, he pulled us back from the brink of disaster and set us on the path we have traveled "to the heights" ever since.

But President Todd was quick to say that he had plenty of help. Equally worthy of our admiration and gratitude is Charles Arthur Robbins, the college's first financial officer, who served as bursar longer (30 years) than Todd served as president (29 years). Todd and Robbins were in effect *partners* in the great enterprise, perfectly aligned in their dedication to the college and their willingness to work hard. Symbolic of Todd's regard for Robbins is the portrait of Robbins that sat on the president's Jones Hall desk, although the corporeal Robbins was himself but a few steps away.

Charles Robbins was born in Indiana in 1881. He and his wife, Bertha Wood, graduated from DePauw University and married in 1906. They immediately joined Bertha's missionary parents in South America, where their three children were born—daughter Rosalie in 1907, and twins Charles Arthur Jr. and Elizabeth in 1910. For 10 years Charles worked as a businessman, five of them in Chili, Peru, and Bolivia. Then in 1911 the family moved to Tacoma.

One day in 1916, in conversation with Edward Todd, Charles Robbins mentioned that he would like to work in education. Todd, still in the process of professionalizing the college's administration, asked Robbins if he would take a job at Puget Sound for the princely annual salary of $900, which was a significant reduction from his income then. Charles thought of the three young children he was trying to raise, talked it over with Bertha, gulped, and accepted Todd's offer. In his history of the college, Todd wrote in characteristic understatement, "His employment proved to be a wise and fortunate move." Robbins was appointed head of the business office (a title soon changed to bursar) and an instructor in Spanish. (He eventually held the rank of associate professor.) By 1939 Charles' annual salary had increased to $3,000. This was augmented by Bertha's $1,000 annual salary as a Spanish instructor at the college.

So what did this guy Robbins do for Puget Sound that was so great? *Everything.* The breadth and variety of responsibilities he bore are unimaginable now, and they came close to ruining him physically. Consider what it must have been like even in a simpler time for him to: run the physical plant, including buying supplies, even for the science labs; do custodial work as required, such as sweeping out the gymnasium and digging trenches for water lines; teach Spanish courses; coach the football team and oh, yes, build the team from nothing; coach the basketball team, ditto; serve as registrar; serve as acting dean of the college (something he did in 1926 when Dean Henry asked to return to the chemistry department); travel with the president on fundraising jaunts; travel across the state to make sure the various farms and ranches owned by the college were managed and operated properly; oversee home mortgages owned by the college and encourage homeowners to make their monthly mortgage payments; serve as switchboard operator as required (the switchboard was located in the bursar's office); be the only person on campus who could keep the master clock (again, located in the bursar's office) running properly; and his main job—bring order to financial management, bookkeeping, accounting, and endowment investment procedures. The college succeeded in those days of scarce operating-money because there were people who did whatever was required to keep the place running. Such is the man the college, and President Todd, had in Charles Robbins.

Prior to 1916 students gave their tuition and fees to the president, the dean, the registrar, or whomever, and, often without proper paperwork or accounting, the money was deposited at the bank. This system proved to be less than satisfactory. (One of the young men entrusted with depositing the funds was good with checks, but not so good with cash. Later, after he was fired and demonstrated a similar personal failing in his next job, he spent several years in the state penitentiary at Walla Walla.) After 1916 proper accounting and annual audits of the books—something that Robbins insisted on—were the order of the day.

When the United States entered World War I, Robbins was in his 30s, too old for military service. He volunteered for the diplomatic service and was sent to Copenhagen. When he returned in 1919 Robbins no longer coached, but he was elected financial secretary of the board of trustees, a post he held for the remainder of his career. At about the same time, Robbins' elderly, retired, missionary parents-in-law came to live with the family in Tacoma until the end of their days. Bertha's father, Thomas Bond Wood, died at age 78 in 1922; her mother, Ellen Dow Wood, at 85 in 1926.

When the college began to scrape an endowment together after the successful fundraising campaigns of 1919–1921, endowment monies were invested in mortgages for Tacoma houses. That is, the college itself lent money to ordinary folk so they could purchase homes. Which worked, but the personal contact with borrowers that was required to keep the mortgage payments coming in on schedule was enormous, and it was the responsibility of Bursar

Robbins. The trustees eventually formed an investment committee and the college got out of the direct mortgage-lending business.

When the Sixth and Sprague campus was no longer adequate for the growing college, it was Todd and Robbins who together tromped around Tacoma and environs searching for a suitable new location. Robbins told a 1931 *Trail* reporter about visiting, with Todd, a Mr. Scott, who lived in the farmhouse that in 1924 became the women's residence for six years, and then the Music Conservatory on the new campus. "We listened to one of the first radios" [in that farmhouse], he said.

Robbins was usually the tallest guy in the room, and he bore himself with authority and dignity. He was respected and admired by those who knew him both inside and outside the college. Robbins in 1937 was one of the founders at Stanford of the Western Association of College and University Business Officers (WACUBO), an organization still going strong today. Robbins served WACUBO as vice president during 1939–1940 and as president in 1940–1941.

In addition to everything else, Robbins was active in the Methodist Church. He served on various conference commissions and was elected lay delegate to the national general conference—held every four years—on eight separate occasions between 1928 and 1956. He later wrote that "this was interesting and took my mind off the college problems." In fact, though, the college itself was hardcore Methodist, and Robbins' Methodist connection was all in the line of duty, even if it was something he enjoyed and believed in.

When Edward Todd retired in 1942, Charles Robbins asked to retire with him. Todd prevailed upon him to stay in the job a while longer to help the new, young president, R. Franklin Thompson, get established. Robbins agreed, but he was tired. The job was still very demanding physically. In fact, gymnasium-sweeping duties frequently still fell to him during the spring of 1944, with the enrollment of 238 Army Specialized Training Program soldiers, many of whom were housed in the gym. The Army required that the gym be spotless.

Charles Robbins finally retired in 1946 at the then-mandatory retirement age of 65. At the same time Bertha retired from teaching. She by then was an assistant professor of Spanish. A reception in their honor was held in Kittredge Hall the evening of September 10, 1946.

Over the years many persons have spent long careers in service to Puget Sound. Few are awarded honorary degrees when they retire. Charles Robbins was so highly regarded after 30 years of service that in 1947 the College of Puget Sound awarded him an honorary doctor of laws degree. Other long-serving persons in this category include Robbins' successor, Gerard Banks, who was bursar for 24 years (1946–1970), and Gwen Phibbs when she and President Philip Phibbs retired.

Charles Robbins passed away in 1967 at age 85. Bertha died the next year. They are buried in Tacoma Cemetery.

We make much of the long-tenured presidents who made the college strong over the past century. But we owe homage as well to their sidekicks, particularly their deans and their financial officers. Here we have remembered the first of the seven financial officers at the college since 1916. In that time five have served for nine years or more—Charles Robbins (30 years), Gerard Banks (24 years), Lloyd Stuckey (nine years), Ray Bell (17 years), and Sherry Mondou (12 years and counting). Strength and stability in this position have been enormously important to Puget Sound's development.

As a footnote to the Robbins' contributions, mention must be made of the *Full Moon Over Cordoba* photograph hanging today in the physics department's outer office. It is a copy of one of the first photographs of the moon, made in 1876 by astronomer Benjamin Apthorp Gould at the Argentine National Observatory, which he founded. Bertha Robbins' missionary father, Thomas Wood, a dedicated amateur astronomer himself, was a friend of Gould's. Gould gave him the photograph. *Full Moon Over Cordoba* hung in the Robbins' Tacoma home for decades before Bertha Robbins gave it to Puget Sound.

1916 College of Puget Sound football team; Robbins is the man in the center. He coached the team in addition to his many other duties, including overseeing the college finances and teaching Spanish courses.

This photo of Robbins was displayed on President Edward Todd's desk for many years (see above facing page).

Charles Arthur Robbins

President Edward H. Todd in his Jones Hall office. Note portrait of Charles Robbins on desk at left, circa 1930.

Charles Robbins was always distinguished and authoritative in his bearing. Here President Edward H. Todd (center) and Robbins (right) accept from Puget Sound National Bank President Reno Odlin, $50,000 in securities from the First Trust.

People of Puget Sound

23. Frances Fullerton Chubb

Art history arrived at Puget Sound in 1926, when the two-semester course History of Art was first offered. By 1935, when Frances Fullerton Chubb matriculated at the College of Puget Sound, the course had been renamed History and Appreciation of Art. Frances probably did not anticipate, when she enrolled in the class her freshman year, that one day she herself would teach it. Nor could she have envisioned the impact she would have on Puget Sound's art department: Frances Chubb stayed at Puget Sound for 41 years. Along the way she *was* art history to thousands of students.

In the fall of 1949, a new course entered the curriculum: Art 77, Understanding the Arts. It was Frances Chubb's creation—"a course designed to bring an increased enjoyment and understanding of the arts of today through lectures, slides, films, and discussions. Contemporary trends in painting, architecture, and sculpture will be stressed, with an attempt being made to answer the most commonly asked questions of 'what and why.'" From the beginning the class attracted a lot of students. Two sections were taught during that first year (1949–50), but by 1959–60 the number had increased to eight, four each semester, all taught by Frances Chubb. The fact that Understanding the Arts counted toward a general education degree requirement for graduation is not enough to explain its enduring popularity. Understanding the Arts was more than a catalog description. It was Miss Chubb's means of inspiring students to care about what they were looking at.

The old History and Appreciation of Art course disappeared after 1952, replaced by new Frances Chubb courses, such as History of Painting, History of Sculpture, and History of Architecture.

Frances served Puget Sound during an era when it was not uncommon for art historians also to be studio artists. Professor Chubb, a painter in watercolors and oils, and an occasional sculptor, taught drawing and painting courses at the beginning of her career. As the department grew and others took these classes over, Frances developed and taught the art history courses. For years she worked hard to carry the department's art history load, until Ron Fields and then others came along to help her out and to expand the department beginning in the late '60s. Bill Colby, while primarily a studio artist, taught the Oriental Art class beginning in the 1960s and throughout his teaching career.

During the solo Chubb years of the 1940s, the art department had few resources and inadequate facilities on the third floor of Jones Hall. By 1950 the department had five faculty members and occupied five rooms in Jones Hall and most of one whole wing of South Hall (razed in 2011). Frances Chubb, in an article giving her much of the credit for that growth, was prescient in her comment to the reporter: "A lot has happened [in the art department] since 1944. But even more is going to happen." She, department chair Lynn Wentworth and, beginning in 1956, Bill Colby, witnessed dramatic growth in the art department, including in its art history component, which has blossomed into today's splendor of offerings that could not have been imagined in 1926 or in 1950.

Frances Chubb was born October 6, 1913, at St. Maries, Idaho, the daughter of William Alonzo Chubb, a machinist, and Myrtle May Fullerton Chubb. William and Myrtle, who married August 30, 1899, at LaCrosse, Wisconsin, had one other child, a daughter, Jeannette, born in 1901. Frances never knew her sister, who died at the age of 2.

In 1905 William and Myrtle lived in Minneapolis, where William worked as a foreman in a railroad roundhouse. By 1910 the pair had settled in Tacoma, except for a brief stint in Idaho. It is not unlikely that William found employment with the Milwaukee Railroad in Northern Idaho, where Frances was born. In any case, the family was in Tacoma in time for William to work at the Todd Shipyards during World War I. After moving around town several times, the family by 1929 had bought a house at 3905 N. 35th St., about a mile north of the Puget Sound campus. This is where Frances lived as a college student and where her parents lived the rest of their lives.

Frances graduated from Tacoma's Stadium High School in 1933. We don't know what occupied her during the next two years, but the Chubbs were Methodists, and it was natural that Frances should enroll in "her" college in 1935, the College of Puget Sound. Frances Chubb made the honor roll her first semester and probably every term thereafter. Throughout her undergraduate career Frances displayed all the energy, enthusiasm, and intelligence of a dedicated college student. She was awarded a Leonard Howarth Scholarship, and she was a member of Pi Gamma Mu, a national honorary for students with scholastic achievement in the social sciences (Frances pursued a sociology minor), and Kappa Phi, the organization of Methodist women students.

During her junior year Frances was secretary of the Art Club, which was preparing for a student exhibit March 6–27, 1938, in Jones Hall to help commemorate the 50th anniversary of the college. The next year, 1938–39, her senior year, Frances served as president of the Art Club and was in charge of publicity for the YWCA in an era when student membership in campus YMCA and YWCA groups was common.

Frances also was elected to Otlah, the senior women's scholastic honorary society. Otlah is today's Mortar Board, which now admits men as well as women. At the end of her senior year

Frances was elected to membership in Mu Sigma Delta, the college's premier scholastic honorary society. As a faculty member Frances maintained her membership in both Otlah/Mortar Board and Mu Sigma Delta, and, for several years in the 1960s, she was faculty advisor to Mortar Board.

Frances graduated from Puget Sound on June 10, 1939, with a Bachelor of Fine Arts degree, with minors in sociology and English literature. The Class of 1939 consisted of 95 graduates, the largest graduating class in the college's history to that time. Frances was one of six graduating magna cum laude.

During 1939–40 Frances enrolled in teacher training courses at Puget Sound and earned a teaching certificate. But rather than teach in the public schools, Frances continued at Puget Sound the next two years as a "fellow in art," a designation that seems to have been created especially for her. She took no classes except for a European history course that she audited. Rather, she served as teaching assistant to the art professors and may have had departmental secretarial duties as well. (During 1941 and 1942 the Tacoma City Directory identified Frances Chubb as an office secretary at the College of Puget Sound.)

But in 1942 Frances became an official instructor in art when art Professor Robert Drummond left to enter military service. Art department Chair Melvin Kohler did the same the year after that, and Frances was the department's only teacher for the next three years, 1943–46. (Kohler returned after the war but stayed only two years before being replaced as chair by Lynn Wentworth.) This was quite a challenge for the young Frances Chubb, but in 1944 Frances added to her workload by beginning a Master of Fine Arts degree program at the University of Washington. She pursued this degree for eight years while teaching at Puget Sound. An M.F.A. in painting was awarded to her in 1952, and with this degree in hand, Frances, in 1953, began climbing the professorial ladder as assistant professor. She was promoted to associate professor in 1958 and to professor in 1968.

Frances Chubb was a charter member of Puget Sound's chapter of the national honorary art fraternity Delta Phi Delta. Established on campus June 4, 1949, the chapter was at the time valued as a means of recognizing outstanding art students. Delta Phi Delta is no longer active.

Frances Chubb sometimes brought into her classes a guest lecturer who was well known to Puget Sound students—Carolyn Schneider, Anderson Hall housemother. "Mrs. Schneider has the best collection of prints in the Northwest," Professor Chubb was quoted as saying in 1952. Carolyn Schneider also was president of the Tacoma Art Association.

As a young person Frances had contracted polio. Throughout her life she wore braces on both legs and on her back. She used crutches to walk. She never complained about the climb to the third floor of Jones Hall, where the art department faculty offices were located. Nor did she complain about teaching classes on the second floor or attending to art exhibitions in the Jones fourth-floor tower art gallery. The stairs to the tower are still among the steepest on campus.

In those days Jones Hall did not have an elevator, nor was the concept of providing accommodations for disabilities given much thought. Professor Emeritus of Art Bill Colby reports that Frances valued her independence and never complained about her daily climb to the heights. But R. Franklin Thompson, president of the college during most of Professor Chubb's tenure as art professor, wrote of his anguish at witnessing the daily struggle she endured climbing the Jones Hall stairways. Despite Frances' unwavering smile and cheerful nature, President Thompson wrote, "I used to silently say, 'Oh, Lord, let me live long enough to give her a classroom on the ground floor.'" In 1960, when Kittredge Hall was remodeled to become the new home of the art department, Frances Chubb finally had an office and a classroom on the first floor.

The classroom was Kittredge 111, occupying space where the soda fountain and the south end of The Commons dining room had been during Kittredge's days as the college student center (1942–59). Kittredge 111 was *the* art history classroom, which meant it was Professor Chubb's classroom. Her office was only a few feet away.

While Professor Chubbs' major contribution was teaching art history, she was also a practicing artist. In 1952 she declared, about her early years as a painter, that "I suppose I considered myself a member of the Ashcan School then. … I was literally painting ashcans." Frances regularly exhibited her work in local and regional art shows through the 1960s. In April 1956 she was elected to membership in Women Painters of Washington, an organization limited to 100 professional women painters whose works had been exhibited in juried shows in the Northwest. Women Painters of Washington, which continues to be active today, was founded in 1930 to help women artists "overcome the limitations they face as women artists and to realize their artistic potential through fellowship."

Travel was difficult for Professor Chubb, but she did strike out on occasion. In the summer of 1949 she visited Arizona, California, Mexico, and several national parks. Back home, she passed along a recommendation: "If you ever go to Indio, Calif., get a date milkshake, they're wonderful." Summer 1965 found her in Puget Sound's Study Afloat program, traveling to Europe and teaching Art 425, Art of the Renaissance and Post-Renaissance Period.

Understanding the Arts was just one of 25 different courses Professor Chubb taught during her 34-year teaching career. During the 27-year period from fall semester 1949 (when Understanding the Arts entered the curriculum) through her retirement, Understanding the Arts was taught 172 times, 167 of those times by Professor Chubb, more than six classes per year on average. During the 1950s, Understanding the Arts averaged 47 students per class. Even if we assume an average enrollment across Professor Chubb's 167 classes of only 40 students per class, we conclude that more than 6,600 students took Understanding the Arts from Professor Chubb. Karen Peterson Finney '67, P'94 was one of them. Karen says of "Miss Chubb" that the course was the single best preparation she had for recognizing, understanding, interpreting, and appreciating the art, architecture, and sculpture she has seen in museums and cathedrals and other buildings throughout her lifetime.

John Delp '64 includes Frances Chubb as an influential professor he remembers fondly. "Not a person who ever took a class from Professor Chubb ever missed a class—who could when she struggled to make it every day without fail? [She was] a living angel," he said.

The 1964 *Tamanawas* was dedicated to Frances Chubb with these words: "Because she is so completely devoted and remains an inspiration to all who know her; because she is justly admired and respected by both young and old; because she continues to give of herself—the students of the University of Puget Sound take great pride in dedicating the 1964 *Tamanawas* to Miss Frances F. Chubb, an outstanding teacher, and wonderful person. We thank you, Miss Chubb, for making the realm of art a fascinating and exciting experience; for rising above the frequent boredom of class routine to a plateau of pleasure; for your gratifying smile ... yes, thank you."

Frances Chubb retired at age 62, at the end of spring semester, 1976. Breathing had become increasingly difficult for her, requiring her to use oxygen. She passed away at age 66, on October 14, 1979. She had never once gone on sabbatical.

Professor Chubb was respected and admired by everyone. Hers was a stable, reliable countenance. Said Emeritus Professor of Art Bill Colby, "She was accepting of others and their opinions. She always contributed. When I wanted critique of my own work, I took it to Frances."

Professor Frances Fullerton Chubb in her third-floor Jones Hall office, 1943.

Frances Fullerton Chubb

Frances Fullerton Chubb, professor of art, Tamanawas, 1954.

Bill Colby

Woodcut print by Emeritus Professor of Art Bill Colby, 1962.

24. Lyle Ford Drushel

During an era when the dean of women was among the college's five most senior administrative officers, the influence of Lyle Ford Drushel was keenly appreciated. Her association with Puget Sound was especially long, beginning in 1907, when she matriculated as a freshman on the old Sixth and Sprague campus, and not ending, really, until she passed away in 1985 at age 97.

Lyle Ford Drushel was born Lyle Elizabeth Ford on September 20, 1888, in Lyons, Nebraska. Her middle name was her mother's first name, a middle name which, by family tradition, Lyle chose for herself. Lyle was the second oldest of four children, three girls and a boy. The Fords moved from Nebraska to Oklahoma and to Kansas, where Lyle graduated from Winfield High School on May 24, 1907. By September the Fords had arrived in Tacoma, where Lyle enrolled at the University of Puget Sound.

Lyle's father was a grocer. Lyle's older sister, Margaretta (1884–1962), worked as a nurse. Lyle's brother, Morris Everett Ford (1894–1958), was an educator in the Parkland, Washington, schools, and in 1948 became the first superintendent of the new Franklin Pierce School District. The Morris E. Ford Middle School is named for him. Its athletic teams are the Ford Thunderbirds.

Lyle lived at home during her college years, at 1105 S. Prospect St., an easy streetcar ride and walk from Sixth and Sprague. The Ford home became a popular hangout for Puget Sound students, especially after Lyle's lively younger sister, Myra Louise (1892–1965), enrolled as a freshman during Lyle's senior year.

While enrolled at Puget Sound, Lyle worked as a teacher in a grammar school. These duties may have been the reason she took a year off between her sophomore and junior years, 1909–10. Lyle graduated in 1912 with honors, when Julius Zeller was president, a year before Edward H. Todd took the helm. For being the graduating senior with "the best knowledge and command of the English language," she was awarded a copy of *Webster's Unabridged Dictionary,* an honor important enough to be noted on her official Puget Sound transcript. Lyle had served as an assistant to the English department for two years. According to a grandnephew, "Her letters written to me during her middle 90s were so lovely that I found myself diagramming her sentences."

After graduating from Puget Sound, Lyle taught school, mostly at Lincoln High School in Tacoma, but also at other places, including Chelan, Washington. Gearing up for World War I, the Selective Service sent Lyle a draft registration form, confused, apparently, by her masculine-sounding name. Regardless, Lyle did spend time during World War I at Astoria, Oregon, where she performed "war camp community service" for the War Department and the Navy Department Commissions on Training Camp Activities. After the war Lyle continued teaching until 1927.

William Allen Drushel (1874–1931) was a chemist and a 1905 graduate of Yale University. He taught at Yale until 1918 and then for the rest of his life worked as a research chemist for Haskelite Manufacturing Corporation in Grand Rapids, Michigan. Allen in 1910 married Pearl Montgomery, with whom he had a daughter, Catherine Anne Drushel (1913–1998). Pearl died in 1923, when Catherine was 10 years old.

Allen Drushel, like Lyle Ford, was educated, outgoing, interesting and interested in life, and attractive and dignified in his personal bearing. Family lore has it that Allen and Lyle met on a train or on a bus traveling to San Francisco for a conference. In any case after a short courtship they married in Tacoma on July

20, 1927. Allen was 53 and Lyle 38. Allen whisked Lyle away to Grand Rapids, where they lived with Catherine.

Tragedy continued to stalk Allen. This time it was he who passed away, of colon cancer, less than four years later, on April 17, 1931. Lyle never remarried. She went by "Lyle Ford Drushel" for the remaining 54 years of her life.

Meanwhile, College of Puget Sound President Edward H. Todd was looking for a new dean of women. Many colleges and universities had started out as all-male institutions. When women began to be admitted, the men who ran the places hired deans of women to segregate as much as possible the women from the men and to "protect" the women and watch out for their interests. Puget Sound enrolled women from the beginning, and during the early years hired matrons or preceptresses. Between 1914 and 1918, for example, Louise Goulder for two years and then Stella Patterson for another two held the title "matron of women's dormitory and preceptress."

In 1922 President Todd hired the first Puget Sound dean of women, Eleanor Brooks Gulick, who also served as head of the English department. Then, between 1922 and 1931, the dean of women position was filled by six different incumbents. It was a difficult time to be a dean of women, with the recent Great War and the social changes it had wrought, the Roaring Twenties, and now the Great Depression roiling up the formerly serene waters of social relations in higher education. Nothing was simple anymore.

President Todd needed stability in the dean of women job. Available for consideration—as the result of personal tragedy—was Lyle Ford Drushel. Todd most certainly knew her from her student days, when he was the college's corresponding secretary, and again later when she was a prominent Tacoma alumna. Whether Todd heard of Allen Drushel's death and wrote to Lyle in Michigan, or whether Lyle returned to Tacoma first, we don't know. But she did move back to Tacoma just a few weeks after Allen died, bringing Catherine with her, and in the fall term of 1931 Lyle Ford Drushel began her 22-year career as Puget Sound's dean of women.

Dean Drushel became one of the very best deans of women to be found anywhere. The qualities she exhibited matched perfectly a description in an October 1933 *Journal of Higher Education* article about "modern" deans of women: tough-minded ("austerely sympathetic"), yet tolerant; able to help mold character by advising with authority on a variety of matters, including course choice, social customs, and vocational fitness. "At a time when everything is in flux, [the dean of women] exerts, in an intimate fashion, a stabilizing influence." It helped that Dean Drushel's demeanor was one of calm and thoughtful deliberation.

In January 1942, when Kittredge Hall opened as the college's first student center, Lyle moved into the dean of women's apartment on the west side of the second floor. The bay window we still see today was in her living room. The window was filled with flowers that Lyle watered as she gazed to the west toward Jones, Howarth, and Anderson halls. (Today the bay window is in the office of art history Professor Zaixin Hong, and the bay window is filled with books, not flowers.)

Lyle also taught in the English department and attained the rank of associate professor. In 1936 New York University awarded her an M.A. degree, which she earned by attending classes in New York during the summer months. Each semester of her Puget Sound career, Lyle taught a freshman composition class and a class in American literature—four courses per year—all while serving as dean.

In 1938 the College of Puget Sound celebrated its 50th anniversary. Dean Drushel wrote to graduates in that year's *Tamana-*

was: "When another 50 years of the life of the college have flashed by, you will be the 'old grads' returning to celebrate the occasion, to welcome former friends and acquaintances, to look with wonder and amazement upon the new college generation of 1988, and to speculate on the future of Puget Sound. What will the world of that day be? What standing will the college have? Will the campus be fully developed and all buildings completed? What will you be like? Who among you will occupy the high places? Who will be famed for contributions to the arts and sciences? The answer to all these questions is shrouded in the mystery of the future. It will be revealed gradually, in time and in degree, as life teaches you loyalty, responsibility, and cooperation. May this Fiftieth Anniversary challenge you to accept your full part in carrying the college forward to worthy achievement!"

Talk about generations coming and going! We can and we do, with 79 years gone since 1938, and we find Dean Drushel's words continue to ring true.

The 1953 *Tamanawas* gives a concise description of Dean Drushel's duties, at the end of her career, in the caption that accompanies her portrait: "Mrs. Lyle Ford Drushel, the Dean of Women, begins her academic year in July as the applications for dormitory space begin to roll in, and ends her year in June as the last woman receives her sheepskin. She keeps an eye on the social calendar, advises Panhellenic, guides sorority rushing, serves as director of Kittredge Hall, and brushes up on notes for her English and literature classes. Her home and office upstairs in the SUB [Student Union Building] has a commanding view of the entire campus where she contends with the occasional blare of the jukebox."

Dean Drushel retired at the end of spring term 1953. She was immediately hauled back to campus to help out as an assistant in the alumni office during 1953–54. But after her brother-in-law Ralph Simpson '13 died in 1954, Lyle went to live with her newly widowed sister, Myra. Myra's grandchildren were also a part of the living mix, and they learned much from and were heavily influenced by their distinguished grandaunt. For example, Lyle taught her grandniece Hattie to drive in Lyle's stick-shift Studebaker. And Lyle guided her grandnephew William toward academic pursuits and a career as a geologist.

Lyle lived for 32 years after she retired. Her primary family caregiver the last few years was her namesake grandniece, Lyle Elizabeth (Libet) Gardner. "When I would take her out for a drive and 'lunch,' she would always indulge her considerable sweet tooth and skip the lunch part. When she was in her 90s, we were in a restaurant, Lyle with a huge chocolate sundae—whipped cream and cherry. She was tiny, bent, and frail looking by that time. A fellow customer came up to me when I paid and said that the sight of Lyle eating that sundae was the cutest thing he had ever seen."

Lyle Ford Drushel died peacefully in a Shelton, Washington, nursing home on December 11, 1985, at age 97, with her niece Betty and grandniece Libet at her side. She is buried in Mountain View Memorial Park, Tacoma.

R. Franklin Thompson knew Dean Drushel well during his years as Puget Sound president (1942–73) and afterward. He wrote about her that she was "an ideal dean of women. She knew what was happening. She had such close contact with the students that they would share their hopes, aspirations, fears, and problems with her. … She was a distinguished-looking person and had beautiful white hair, which on rare occasions had a blue tint after she had been to a beauty parlor. The students affectionately called her 'Blue Dru.'"

Students dedicated the 1939 *Tamanawas* to Lyle Ford Drushel, declaring "her influence has helped many realize dreams of ideal college life. Her contact with both men and women students has inspired cherished acquaintances." The caption on Dean Drushel's portrait in the 1943 *Tamanawas* is: "… gracious and charming—anyone's picture of a dean of women."

College of Puget Sound Dean of Women and Associate Professor of English Lyle Ford Drushel '12 waters her plants in her Kittredge Hall apartment, 1952. The location of the apartment can be identified by the bay window that still exists today on the second floor of the Lawrence Street side of Kittredge Hall.

People of Puget Sound

Lyle Elizabeth Ford Drushel, College of Puget Sound dean of women, Tamanawas *1937*.

Campus Day, University of Puget Sound, Sixth and Sprague campus, 1908. Standing with a nice smile at the right of the third row from the front is Lyle Elizabeth Ford '12, who, as Lyle Ford Drushel, served as Puget Sound's dean of women between 1931 and 1953. This photograph appears on page 143 (and also on page 133) of Lyle Elizabeth Ford's School Girl Days, A Memory Book, *Mss. 055*.

Lyle Ford Drushel

Lyle Elizabeth Ford '12, back row third from right, with unidentified fellow UPS students on an outing to Fox Island, March 1911. This photograph appears on page 144 of Lyle Elizabeth Ford's School Girl Days, A Memory Book, *Mss. 055.*

Lyle Elizabeth Ford '12, left, with unidentified fellow UPS student on an April canoeing outing to American Lake. This photograph appears on page 146 of Lyle Elizabeth Ford's School Girl Days, A Memory Book, *Mss. 055 in university archives.*

People of Puget Sound

25. Students' Army Training Corps

After the United States entered World War I in 1917, the War Department created the Students' Army Training Corps (SATC). The program helped to stem and control what had become a rapid departure of male students from college campuses. The War Department wanted men to remain enrolled until they were needed. The SATC program therefore worked for the benefit of the colleges and the war effort. Hundreds of colleges across the nation, including the College of Puget Sound, were certified by the War Department to establish SATC groups of a minimum of 100 men.

A large photograph shows 92 of the students enrolled in the College of Puget Sound SATC, as well as some 20 workmen building the barracks the government required the college to construct. Taken in 1918 by longtime Tacoma photographer Marvin Boland, the original photograph is 6.6 inches high by 19.5 inches wide. To the right of the barracks, out of the photograph, was the main building of the college at the Sixth Avenue and Sprague campus. (The college moved to its present location in 1924.)

Fall semester 1918 was the first term of study for Puget Sound men in the program. The men were inducted into the Army on October 1, 1918, and were paid as privates while engaged in their studies. Because the SATC men lived together in the barracks, they were likely candidates to contract the deadly influenza that was sweeping the country, and 30 of them did. Beginning on October 10, 1918, classes for all CPS students were suspended because of the flu outbreak. All of the SATC men survived, but three women students died.

The SATC was short-lived. On November 11, 1918, the armistice was signed, and in December 1918 the SATC program ended across the country. The new barracks became the college's gymnasium. The trustees had insisted the barracks be built with a truss roof rather than with posts—despite the added cost—so that the building could serve this purpose after the war.

Students' Army Training Corps men at their barracks under construction on Puget Sound's Sixth and Sprague campus, 1918.

26. Warren Everett Tomlinson

William Homer Maris, the composer of Oregon State University's alma mater, was a popular professor of German at the College of Puget Sound and had been for three years when, in 1933, he collided on his bicycle with an automobile and perished. The campus grieved.

College teaching jobs for German professors were scarce in 1933, but with Professor Maris' untimely death, one had just opened up. A last-minute exchange of letters brought Warren Everett Tomlinson on the run from his father's farm outside Hutchinson, Minnesota, to the Chicago, Milwaukee, St. Paul and Pacific Railroad's station 14 miles away at Glencoe, where he hopped aboard *The Olympian*, which was carrying Puget Sound President Edward Todd eastward. Tomlinson listened to Todd extoll the virtues of the Pacific Northwest, Tacoma, and the College of Puget Sound. With five minutes to go before the train's arrival in Minneapolis, where Tomlinson was to get off, Todd "pulled out his little notebook and asked me rapid fire about six or eight questions that you should ask on such an interview," Tomlinson told President R. Franklin Thompson 46 years later.

Tomlinson, with a new Ph.D. from the University of Berlin, got the job. He joined the faculty in fall 1933 as associate professor of German. In 1966 he told me, "I was over there in Germany teaching and decided it was probably getting close to the time to leave the place, the way things were deteriorating politically. And with a worldwide economic recession raging, I figured if I wanted to get a college teaching job, I had better have a Ph.D. degree, so I got one."

Tomlinson was born November 14, 1902, the youngest of six children. He told a *Trail* reporter in 1950 of trudging through raging Minnesota blizzards and minus-20-degree temperatures the three miles from the farm to town to attend high school. In 1924 he received a bachelor's degree from Carleton College. Then, at age 22, Warren Tomlinson began a lifelong career as a globetrotter. He was in Hong Kong on his college graduation day, then for the next three years taught in the Philippines and traveled and hiked throughout China, Japan, Malaysia, Burma, and India. But he was just warming up. In 1927 he made his way to Germany.

There Tomlinson accepted a job teaching English in a school for ordinary citizens, the Berlin Evening College, which was something new in Germany. He stayed in this job for five years. Because he taught evenings, his days were free, and he began taking courses at the University of Berlin.

Tomlinson returned to the United States in 1932 with the Ph.D. (the degree was actually awarded in 1933) and a beautiful wife. In Germany, as in most of Europe, professors resided atop pedestals, and interactions with students were quite formal. But when Jeanette Blumenthal-Knoll enrolled in one of Tomlinson's classes, the status distinction between them quickly became secondary. One day Warren and Jeanette passed on the stairway, one going up, the other down. Both turned to look back. Something sizzled. They married on May 14, 1932.

Jeanette was seven years younger than Warren, born in Storozynetz, Austria. This part of Austria became part of Romania in 1918 and was occupied by the Nazis in 1940.

Tomlinson with his bride spent the 1932–33 academic year at his family's farm looking for work, except during their 23-day hitchhiking jaunt around Minnesota that cost the newlyweds a total of $18. Hitchhiking was fun, but the elegant Jeanette did not enjoy the icy Minnesota winter. Fortunately, she did not have to endure another, thanks to President Todd's offer of a job.

Hitler took over Germany six months after Warren and Jeanette left the country. Said Tomlinson in 1947, "I lived five blocks from the palace where all the political rallies were held, yet I never saw Hitler. He was so low no respectable person would go to one of his meetings." In 1935 Jeanette's mother, Regina Knoll, who was Jewish, left Germany and came to Tacoma to live with Warren and Jeannette. The certainty in the family was that this move saved her life.

The Tomlinsons had two daughters, Barbara and Vivian. The Tomlinsons lived for decades in a rented home at 1414 North 5th St. (monthly rent in 1940: $45). Tomlinson rented because he did not wish to own a house, he declared to me in 1966. Being tied down by home ownership did not fit with his traveling lifestyle. "Money is for going places and doing things," he said. According to the 1940 census, Tomlinson's 1939 income was $2,600.

Colleagues and students called him "Tommy." He taught history and political science, as well as German. Students flocked to his classes as his reputation for intellectual rigor, high energy, and enthusiastic delivery grew. He sang German folk songs and made his students sing them as well. Two that I still remember word-for-word 50 years later are *Du, du, ligest mir im Herzen*, and *Mein Hut der hat drei Ecken*.

Tomlinson was passionately committed to developing in his students an interest in world affairs. Political Science 121, Current National and International Problems, was one of his most popular courses. A tool that he used both to stimulate students' thinking and to measure their views was the world affairs opinion survey he regularly made up and administered in his classes. He reported the results campuswide. In response to the question on a spring 1952 survey, "Should the U.S. recognize the Chinese Communist government after all hostilities cease in the Korean war?" 35 students said "yes," 60 said "no," and 14 "don't know."

The International Relations Club was one of the most active student organizations on campus from the 1920s into the 1960s. After Tomlinson's good friend, history and political science Professor Frank G. Williston, left Puget Sound for the University of Washington in 1943, Tommy became the IRC faculty advisor. Under his guidance, the IRC sponsored campus events and hosted regional and national conferences of international relations clubs.

Tomlinson spoke frequently about world affairs, both on and off campus. On one occasion after a summer of traveling, he described in weekly chapel Europeans' worry that U.S. hysteria over communism would lead the country to stumble blindly into World War III. Tommy also inherited from Williston what they both jokingly called "the PTA circuit" of talks and lectures. Tommy was one of the most knowledgeable people in Tacoma about world affairs and he was in high demand as a speaker. He had traveled so extensively that, beginning in 1943, he delivered orientation lectures to Fort Lewis soldiers about to be posted overseas. In October 1950 Tomlinson received the Tacoma NAACP award for being "the local citizen who during the year has made the most notable contribution in the field of improved human relations."

In the summer of 1951 Tomlinson teamed up with Christian Miller to put on a summer school session in Sweden. Tommy (with Jeanette, Barbara, and Vivian) led a group of 36 CPS students and faculty, with spouses, through Portugal, Italy, Switzerland, France, Germany, and Denmark on the way to Gothenburg for the four-week session of classes in English. Finally heading for home, the four Tomlinsons departed Southhampton on September 1 on the ship *MV Neptunia*, arriving in New York on September

11, just in time to scoot back to Tacoma for the beginning of fall semester. Throughout the 1950s, Warren and Jeanette organized and led travel groups abroad.

Warren Tomlinson's beloved Jeanette died of cancer at age 51, on January 29, 1961. Rather than rattling around by himself in his house on 5th Street, Tomlinson began providing accommodations for Puget Sound international students. Throughout the 1960s the house was full of them, sort of an international residence hall. Many of these students were more than happy later to reciprocate by putting up their old prof when he visited their countries.

During the spring semester of 1966 Tomlinson teamed up with philosophy Professor John Magee to lead Puget Sound's first semester-study-abroad for 40 Puget Sound honors students, including my wife Karen and me, in Vienna, Austria. We took our degree-credit courses from Tomlinson and Magee at the Pension Andreas, and sat in on courses at the University of Vienna. Studying European history in Vienna with Warren Tomlinson and gadding about with him to look at what we were studying made for a rich experience.

Two 1966 memories of Warren Tomlinson: (1) being rescued by him after I unwisely photographed the Red Army in Hungary (see "*My Life as a Cold War Spy*," page 203), and (2) Karen and I spending spring break in Salzburg and busing to St. Gilgen am Wolfgangsee, 30 kilometers east, to rendezvous with Tomlinson for a hike around the lake and a cable car ride up the Zwölferhorn. Tommy declared more than once he could teach a student as much while traveling as he could in the classroom, and he sure could.

Tommy continued to lead Puget Sound semester study-abroad groups, including during summers. President Thompson referred to Warren Tomlinson as Puget Sound's "ambassador-at-large," an appropriate title for the man who helped launch study abroad as an integral component of a Puget Sound education.

After retiring in 1973 at age 70, Tommy continued his world travels. A letter to Karen and me dated February 19, 1975, describes a typical Tomlinson solo trip abroad: four months in Japan and the South Seas. In Japan he stayed at the home of former Puget Sound student, Kiseko Miki, whose father, Takeo Miki, was just being installed as Japan's new prime minister. In the South Seas Tommy wrote of "scenes of desperate fighting in World War II, with wrecks and debris still lying around. The best experience there was in the Marshall Islands, a 10-day field trip on a ship taking supplies to outer islands, and picking up their valuable copra. Dirty ship and rough seas, but still a good trip. Met people and saw how they really live—not in the towns. Met many Peace Corps boys." He finished with, "Might go to Vienna this summer and take a trip down the Danube on a Russian boat."

Warren Tomlinson passed away in Tacoma at age 78 on January 11, 1981. Those of us who knew and loved him were sad, of course. And we were surprised. We thought he would live forever. Tommy was always on the move.

Professor Warren E. Tomlinson on the cover of the October 6, 1950, issue of The Trail.

International Relations Club advisor Professor Warren E. Tomlinson with three of the new foreign students enrolled fall semester 1950. From left to right: Frank Costanza from Italy, Kuros Amuzdar from Iran, Professor Tomlinson, and Peter Borner from Germany. They are relaxing at the Top of the Ocean Restaurant after the Tuesday, October 3, 1950, banquet of the International Relations Club. According to the October 6, 1950, issue of The Trail, *page 6, "The International Relations Club is composed of students from foreign countries and from the U.S. who are interested in world relations."*

Professor Tomlinson gesturing in class, 1963. (University Bulletin *1963-64/1964-65).*

People of Puget Sound

Professor Warren Tomlinson points out some of the wonders of Paris to Anne Alworth '67 (partially hidden) and Diane "Dee Dee" Dressel '67 from atop the Arc De Triomph in Paris, France, February 13, 1966. After spending a week each in London, Paris, and Rome, the University of Puget Sound semester study abroad group landed in Vienna for the remainder of the spring 1966 semester.

Diane Garland '67 looks on as John Finney '67 presents Professor Warren E. Tomlinson, faculty leader (with Professor John B. Magee) of the University of Puget Sound 1966 Vienna semester study abroad group, a book on Albrecht Durer's paintings in appreciation for his leadership and support throughout the semester. Taken at the Commencement dinner (for the five seniors in the group; the rest were juniors) at the Palais Palffry, Vienna Austria, 1966.

1966 Vienna study abroad group on tour at the Schwechat Brewery in Vienna. Those in the photograph include Professor Warren Tomlinson (center, with white hair) and 24 of the 40 members of the study abroad group. Seated, from left: Georgia Depue, Janet McClellan, Betty Blanchard, Karen Finney, Liz Watson, Mary Margaret Hillier, Lexi Otto, Rod Johnson, and Al Howe. Standing: Don Taylor, Gordon Cook, Al Campbell, Al Nordell, Gary Birchler, John Finney, David Wagner, Jim Nelson, Warren Tomlinson, Larry Nicholson, unidentified brewery tour guide, Gerard Kern, Larry Otto, Russ McCurdy, Robert Sprenger, Jr., Johnny Johnston, and (in dark glasses), an unidentified brewery tour guide.

Professor Warren E. Tomlinson in class. (Tamanawas, *1967*).

Places of Puget Sound

27. Deep Creek Lodge

When World War II ended, the College of Puget Sound enrolled a great many war veterans whose presence changed the campus climate in positive ways. Many of those young men had shouldered huge responsibilities during the war, and in college they were eager for outdoor physical recreational opportunities to complement their classroom studies. Such opportunities were enhanced greatly when, in June 1948, the Associated Students of the College of Puget Sound (ASCPS) acquired Deep Creek Lodge, located 60 miles east of Tacoma on the north side of Highway 410.

The drive to acquire Deep Creek Lodge came from members of the men's ski team, coached by Professor of Chemistry Robert Sprenger, himself an avid skier. Teams from rival colleges with such facilities enjoyed a competitive advantage over Puget Sound skiers, who had to return to Tacoma each day at the end of practice. Ski team members Chuck Howe B.A.'50, B.E.'51 and Clint Gossard '51 therefore began looking for a cabin close to where the team practiced at Cayuse Pass, near the northeast corner of Mount Rainier National Park.

Phil Gossard, Clint's father and White River sales manager for Weyerhaeuser, suggested that Chuck and Clint contact Nevan McCullough, ranger for the Forest Service's White River District, which included Snoqualmie National Forest, outside park boundaries. McCullough knew of a site the skiers could look at, a public tourist camp located on Deep Creek, owned by a man who was about to lose his lease with the Forest Service. The ski team wanted a cabin, but this was something else altogether—a 13-acre facility with two lodges and seven cabins. The owner wanted $6,500 for his buildings, and McCullough told the students he thought the college would be successful if it sought a lease on the land.

Although the possibility of obtaining a recreational facility to serve the entire campus—rather than a cabin just for the ski team—was a new idea, Professor Sprenger had no hesitation in approaching President R. Franklin Thompson, who gave his support. Chuck Howe spoke with ASCPS's central board, which was likewise enthusiastic. The opportunity to lease 13 acres and to purchase the buildings seemed too good to pass up, and the deal was made. Beyond its use by skiers, both President Thompson and ASCPS felt that Deep Creek could serve as the locus for student outdoor activities all year long.

Professor Sprenger, ski team members, and student volunteers went right to work to whip Deep Creek Lodge (as ASCPS officially named the facility) into shape. Over the next 12 months they converted one of the cabins into a small shower and lavatory building. They installed bunk beds, increasing capacity to eight to 10 people per cabin. They built a septic system and a gravity-fed water system. One of the lodges became a permanent caretaker's home, while the other became a recreational center. A small powerhouse supplied electricity. A corduroy log road was constructed leading up to a 60-by-100-foot body of water that students and Professor Sprenger cleaned of debris for an ice skating pond. All of this work was completed by student volunteers. Chuck Howe, a surgical technician aboard attack personnel ships in the Navy, had seen action on Iwo Jima and Okinawa. For him and other war veterans, attacking deficiencies at Deep Creek Lodge was easy duty by comparison.

Because Deep Creek Lodge was considered part of the College of Puget Sound campus, social rules there were the same as for the main campus in Tacoma. A November 1948 issue of *The Trail* published the "Use Rules for Deep Creek." These included the expectation there would be no "mixed visiting" between cabins. Steve and Jerry Stevenson served as Deep Creek's full-time caretakers from 1948 until June 1951. This husband-and-wife team acted as chaperones, permitting men and women to use Deep Creek Lodge. (Steve, whose weight fell from 190 pounds to 90 pounds during the Bataan Death March, claimed that the outdoor life and hard work at Deep Creek Lodge contributed to his physical recovery after the war.) Lights went off at 11 p.m., when the Stevensons turned off the power plant. Firewood was not to be chopped inside the cabins. Deep Creek itself was not to be polluted, for which offense the U.S. Forest Service would impose a $25 fine.

The same issue of *The Trail* published the "Operating Policy of Deep Creek." The overnight capacity of Deep Creek was 60 persons. Reservations no more than one week in advance must be made in person at the office of bursar Gerard Banks, where a list was maintained. In order to receive overnight accommodations at Deep Creek a student had to present to the Stevensons a reservation receipt issued by the Bursar's office. Students could invite up to two non-student guests, and student organizations could use Deep Creek. But "during the ski season, overnight accommodations by a single organization shall be limited to two-thirds of the capacity of the area, or 40 people, on Saturday nights." These operational rules anticipated heavy student demand for use of the Deep Creek facilities, although the rules were relaxed in later years when demand declined.

The story of Deep Creek is also the story of a student group called the Chinook Club, which was created by ASCPS in September 1948 to oversee management of Deep Creek. ASCPS took pains to make it clear that Deep Creek belonged to all students, not just to Chinook members. But the degree to which Deep Creek succeeded and the degree to which the Chinook Club functioned well paralleled each other very closely over the period between 1948 and 1956. In the early years, Chinook's members were heavily committed to the success of Deep Creek Lodge. Chuck Howe became student recreation manager, and Professor Sprenger was recreation advisor. Together, these two had primary responsibility for operations at Deep Creek Lodge. To drum up interest among the student body, the Chinook Club held an open house at Deep Creek each fall semester through 1955. The first open house was on Sunday, October 31, 1948. Transportation from campus was provided, departing at 9 a.m. and returning at 6 p.m. Despite rain that day, some 100 students attended.

From the beginning, much of the work of maintaining the Deep Creek buildings fell to students. Some work was performed by the Stevensons and later by their successors, Mr. and Mrs. Wilkins. The buildings were located in deep woods beneath tall trees in a damp climate, and they were heated by wood stoves. Cajoling student volunteers to chop firewood was an ongoing campaign of the Chinook Club. Even though much firewood was split during the summer of 1948, Deep Creek users ran out of firewood before winter's end that year and had eventually to saw and chop outside in the cold.

Heavy snow fell throughout the winter of 1948–49. Although the Forest Service had logged an area adjacent to Deep Creek Lodge that could be used for skiing, the elevation was only 2,700 feet, too low for early or reliable snowfall. Instead, the ski team practiced and held meets at Cayuse Pass (elevation 4,800 feet), some 10 miles east of Deep Creek Lodge. There, ski team members sought to install a rope tow. Bob Johnson, aide to Mount Rainier National Park Ranger Pat Patterson, had responsibility for the Cayuse-Tipsoo area in the northeast corner of the park. Johnson was a veteran of the Army's 10th Mountain Division, which served in Italy, and was an exceptionally accomplished skier. Sympathetic to the wishes of CPS skiers, Johnson gave them permission to install a rope tow inside the park boundary, near Tipsoo Lake. Wrote Chuck Howe years later, "Johnson gave CPS verbal permission to build a tow at Cayuse, simple as that! No paperwork or long wait for a request to go through government channels." The ski team was prohibited from cutting trees and had to remove the tow equipment from the park at the end of each ski season. A war surplus Allis-Chalmers engine that President Thompson helped to acquire for the college powered the tow.

This facility, in combination with overnight accommodations at Deep Creek Lodge, gave the ski team the resources it was looking for. Skiing was just beginning its upward climb in popularity, and the College of Puget Sound became a leader in the Pacific Northwest in generating interest. Each February, Professor Sprenger took the CPS ski team to Banff, Alberta, Canada, to participate in international competition. Two months after the 1950 competition, skiers assembled at Deep Creek Lodge to view a film made at the Banff event. They also viewed a film about the Corral Pass ski area proposed for development adjacent to Deep Creek Lodge, with a chairlift going some 3,000 feet higher up the mountain. This was an exciting possibility, indeed.

In the spring semester of 1949, the college's physical education department began offering beginner, intermediate, and advanced ski instruction courses for credit. The college was able to hire as ski instructors Martin Fopp and Shirley McDonald Fopp '41. Martin Fopp was a Swiss ski team racer who emigrated to the U.S. in 1940. He won the U.S. Downhill Championship in 1942, and Shirley won the '42 Women's Combined. They had taught at Sugar Bowl, California, Big Bromley, Vermont, and Jackson Hole, Wyoming. According to Howe, their "hiring created great attention in the Northwest ski world." Most instruction took place at Cayuse Pass, although some instruction occurred at Deep Creek Lodge after a rope tow became operational there in January 1952. The Fopps gave ski instruction each weekend for 15 weeks, and students had to attend 10 of the 15 sessions to pass the course. The Fopps offered the ski course through 1956.

The Trail acknowledged in a December 1948 editorial the contribution of Professor Sprenger to the reinvigorated outdoor recreation program: "Hats off to Dr. Sprenger; The new ski school to be established here is the direct result of his untiring work. … Dr. Sprenger has devoted much time to the development of Deep Creek, and the whole recreation program. … The administration is backing Dr. Sprenger's plan. Here is the chance for students to get excellent ski instruction and also get credit for it."

One student who took the ski class, Nahad Askari, broke his foot and injured his knee during the March 20, 1949, class. After being driven to Tacoma General Hospital and subsequently released with his foot in a cast, Mr. Askari declared, "The first thing I can do I shall go skiing again." Mr. Askari was a CPS student from Iraq.

Each February for several years the Chinook Club sponsored a winter carnival. The first of these, called "Bahnfrei," occurred the weekend of February 12 and 13, 1949. Six students vied for the title of Snow Queen: Rae Jeanne Neeley '52; Lois Leland '51; Jean Gudmundson '50; Dorothy Schweinler 'B.A.'46, B.E.'49; Delores

Breum '51; and Lorayne Willoughby '64. Only men were allowed to vote. They elected Jean Gudmundson, who was identified as "an oddity among ski queens, one who can ski." Each year as part of the carnival, an intramural giant slalom race was held at Cayuse Pass. In 1949 it was won by the Kappa Sigma fraternity men and by independent (non-Greek) women.

The Chinook Club's 1950 winter carnival began on February 22, George Washington's birthday, a Wednesday holiday on which no classes were held. At the Cayuse ski area Gloria Christiansen '48 was crowned Snow Queen. Chris Ostrom '53 broke her ankle during the races. Professor Sprenger presented awards to race winners at Friday night's winter carnival dance in Kittredge Hall, then the student center on campus. The next day, Saturday, a snow sculpting contest was held at Deep Creek Lodge. A sculpture of Donald Duck won. That evening students square danced in the lodge. The weekend ended on Sunday with a pancake-eating contest.

The Chinook Club's February 1951 Winter Ski Festival featured a Ski King, rather than a Snow Queen. Ski King Bill Goettling '54 served with an all-male court. After the February 25 races at Cayuse Pass, won by Sigma Chi, the campus bus took skiers back to Deep Creek Lodge, where they "warmed themselves and had free pie and coffee."

Aside from the winter carnivals, Deep Creek Lodge was in those early years the location of choice for the activities of many student and non-student groups. For example, a ski party was held at Deep Creek Lodge the weekend of February 26–27, 1949, for independent students. Activities included "skiing, snow fights, eating, and dancing." Typical of non-student use was the December 1949 Pacific Northwest Ski Association instructors' certification program, relocated from Stevens Pass for lack of snow there.

Although events like these were successful, Deep Creek Lodge never did become a financially self-sustaining operation. After the big wave of war veterans graduated, student use of the facility declined. The arduous annual tasks of maintaining the cabins and chopping firewood appealed to students less and less. At the February 23, 1956, meeting of ASCPS's central board, Professor Sprenger laid out the stark realities. Deep Creek revenues were about $1,000 per year, but expenses ran about $2,000. Use of Deep Creek Lodge was increasingly being made by outside groups, not by students.

Said Sprenger, "When ASCPS purchased Deep Creek eight years ago, the lodge was well used. Since that time, however, student interests have turned elsewhere. The number of CPS students per weekend using Deep Creek has dwindled to one or two." Although outside groups booked the lodge almost every weekend, the rates that could be charged for the primitive facilities did not cover costs. Professor Sprenger advised ASCPS that students should either use Deep Creek or dispose of it. Student leaders, after appointing a committee to review the situation, decided to sell the facility. The process of finding a buyer who could meet Forest Service lease requirements began, and the sale of Deep Creek Lodge was final in 1957. The college received $6,500, the same amount it had paid in 1948.

In September 1956 *The Trail* wrote, in an editorial titled "Farewell to Deep Creek," that Deep Creek was "a noble experiment" that had worked in the immediate postwar years, but now, with mainly non-student users, was operating as a money-losing "hotel as a public relations gesture for the college." Concluded *The Trail*, " … it is sad to watch the end of a possibility-laden project like Deep Creek." In March 1957 *The Trail* wrote, "in selling Deep Creek, the ASCPS removed a millstone from its collective neck."

Retired sociology professor and associate academic Dean Frank Peterson '50 has memories of Deep Creek Lodge. "It was very popular with the students who wanted to ski for the weekend. The lodge and log cabins, located among the fir trees, were quite well constructed but were pretty primitive. Although it was a quaint place, maintenance was a real problem. It needed care that the students could not provide and, after the 'newness' wore off, use declined markedly. Decay, dampness, and vandalism were continual problems. It was a beautiful setting, but the distance from campus and the costs were too great."

In 1980 former President R. Franklin Thompson reminisced about Deep Creek. He wrote, "On several occasions Lucille and I went up for the day, watched [the students] ski, and always had a potluck dinner in the evening. I shall never forget the fireplace in the [lodge] smoked and you not only had picnic food but you also had barbecued food."

Sally Sprenger is the middle child (of three) of Professor Robert Sprenger and Mae Sprenger. During the time she served as international student coordinator in Puget Sound's Office of International Programs, Sally spoke of Deep Creek vividly, saying, "I grew up there. My parents liked to say that I learned to ski before I learned to walk." The Sprenger family visited Deep Creek year-round. In the summer the Sprengers stayed for longer periods, hiking and picking huckleberries. Some years they celebrated Thanksgiving at Deep Creek. After Deep Creek was sold, Sally and her family cried every time they drove by. "It was so cool to be a faculty kid and to be able to go there."

The vast ski facility planned for Corral Pass never materialized, but Crystal Mountain did, opening on December 1, 1962. The College of Puget Sound's Deep Creek Lodge is today's Alta Crystal Resort, considerably improved. Outside of Crystal Mountain's own facilities, Alta Crystal provides the only overnight accommodations in the area. On occasion the university has used Alta Crystal Resort for group meetings and retreats.

Students relaxing by the fire at Deep Creek Lodge, November 1953.

Deep Creek Lodge

Caretaker's cabin at Deep Creek, winter 1949.

This image appears on page 35 of the 1949 Tamanawas with this caption: "Deep Creek and snowy mountain slopes become the setting for ski classes in Physical Education as this group prepares to master the art."

Places of Puget Sound

Deep Creek Lodge.

Professor Robert Sprenger (lower right) and seven members of the CPS ski team at the intercollegiate international competition at Banff Alberta, February 1950. Chuck Howe is to Professor Sprenger's right.

Deep Creek Lodge

Annual chore: splitting firewood at Deep Creek, 1949.

CPS Cayuse Pass rope tow in operation, 1949.

Places of Puget Sound

A Puget Sound student skis on highway 410 from Deep Creek Lodge to the CPS Cayuse Pass ski area, 1949.

Puget Sound ski team members Joe Hedges M.S. '49, P'72,'73 and Bob Morrison '50 on the ridge next to the CPS Cayuse Pass ski area near Deep Creek Lodge, circa 1949.

Deep Creek Lodge

Sign at the entrance to Deep Creek Lodge on U.S. Highway 410, 1949.

CPS truck used for work at the ski team's Cayuse Pass ski area and at Deep Creek Lodge, circa 1949.

Places of Puget Sound

28. University Place
The Campus that Almost Was

Did the city of University Place really get its name from the University of Puget Sound?

The answer is, yes. University Place was born by a vote of the Puget Sound University trustees on August 10, 1893. For 10 years thereafter the university and the place were inextricably linked, for better, for worse, for richer, for poorer, until they parted.

After it was incorporated in 1888, our college bounced around among several locations in Tacoma, trying to settle on a home. A campus plan that bubbled up in 1893 finally seemed to offer a good chance for success: building on undeveloped land west of the city, and funding the project by the sale of residential lots surrounding the campus. The plan failed, but not for lack of trying.

Here is what happened. In 1893, after two years of the college leasing its first building to Tacoma schools, large mortgage payments were due that could not be paid. At the April 5, 1893, Puget Sound University trustee meeting, sale of the building was approved and several proposals for an alternative campus location were made. Two seemed promising—one at Gravelly Lake and the other on the Tacoma Narrows, including what was known as Lemon's Beach.

Because construction of a streetcar line to Gravelly Lake could not be guaranteed, the trustees accepted the Tacoma Narrows offer of a gift of lands and options to purchase adjacent lands. At the same time—August 10, 1893—on the suggestion of Chancellor Crawford Thoburn and by vote of the trustees, the name University Place was chosen for the residential community. A planned extension of Division Avenue, as well as streetcar service, would connect University Place to Tacoma.

Once platted, residential lots available for sale at University Place numbered in the thousands. To get out from under the burden of managing the real estate business themselves, PSU trustees on April 17, 1894, created the University Land Company to hold the land and to sell the lots. In October the first lots were priced at $100, but this was reduced to $50 the next April.

Publicity brochures give a bird's-eye view of the proposed campus, which was to occupy "not less than sixty acres" at the center of University Place. Planned buildings included a main administration and classroom building, separate women's and men's residence halls, a museum, a library, a gymnasium, and, eventually, separate buildings for law, medicine, art, and manual training. A chapel was to stand opposite the main building. Residential land around the campus was to be platted "as a whole and in harmony with" the "bold treatment" of campus land, "aiming at a grand perspective."

"The grounds command a fine view of Puget Sound and its islands, with the Coast ranges and Olympic mountains in the background. The scenery, together with the fishing, bathing and boating would make such a location a very successful summer resort."

Who would not want to attend a college in such a location?

The architect for campus buildings at University Place was George Wesley Bullard (1856–1935), a local who had designed Tacoma's First Congregational Church and Engineering Hall on the University of Illinois campus at Urbana-Champaign. For University Place buildings, Bullard chose the French Gothic style, with slate roofs, copper metalwork, and superstructures "faced with buff-colored pressed brick, with trimmings of light-colored terra cotta."

Construction cost estimates were $80,000 for the main building, $40,000 for the ladies' hall, $35,000 for the men's hall, and $20,000 for the heating and lighting plant. Had all of the lots sold, the initial $175,000 campus construction cost would have been reached many times over.

Development of University Place lands was to be governed by modern principles of landscape architecture. The University Land Company in 1895 hired Edward Otto Schwagerl (1842–1910) to oversee and manage the design and development of UP lands. Schwagerl had been Tacoma's park superintendent from 1890 to 1892 and Seattle's from 1892 to 1895. He designed Tacoma's Wright Park and was involved in the design of Point Defiance Park. In Seattle he redesigned Denny Park and oversaw completion of Kinnear Park. In selecting Schwagerl, trustees had picked a man described as being at the top of his profession, "with no superior in the United States."

Schwagerl wrote in the December 1895 issue of the student newspaper *The University Record* (known also as *Ye Recorde*) about the land he was responsible for developing: "The ground embraces an area of some 1,200 acres. It is by no means a level piece of ground being in a general tendency of a gently rolling nature, which is more or less broken by its ridges and charming valleys. … The boulevard, linking University Place with the City of Tacoma, is made possible with most satisfactory conditions of grade alignment and curvatures, the same entering the University grounds naturally and in a very happy manner."

The boulevard was Division Avenue, a project of The Division Avenue Extension and Improvement Company, whose president was Tacoma mayor and PSU trustee Ira Towne, and whose landscape architect was Schwagerl himself. Division Avenue ended (and still does) at the intersection of Sixth and Sprague—ironically, Puget Sound's campus location from 1903 to 1924. An almost straight-line extension of Division Avenue from that point would have brought Division directly to the proposed campus at University Place.

In a later *Ye Recorde* article, Schwagerl worked himself up to a fever pitch of enthusiasm, writing about "The Puget Sound Arboretum or Museum of Trees" that he would create on 200 of the best acres for growth and preservation of some 250 varieties. He wrote of the Olmstead-designed Arnold Arboretum at Harvard and declared that PSU trustees would create at University Place a museum to surpass even that. Schwagerl wrote that the arboretum would open "a large field for practical study, investigation, and experiment which will be seconded by the additional departments of Botany, horticulture and agriculture."

Students were thrilled about their new campus. From the January 15, 1896, issue of *Ye Recorde:*

"It is the plan to commence the erection of the elegant new buildings in the near future, and in every respect the outlook for the new University is most satisfactory.

"As students we are looking with pleasure to the time when we shall occupy our new buildings, and possess our own athletic field, gymnasium, etc. And we believe our fondest hopes will be realized."

But such cheerful anticipation was not matched by fiscal reality. Money from the sale of lots was simply not forthcoming in amounts necessary to construct the campus. University Land Company practices and a severe economic recession undermined the ultimate objective. Commissions to sales agents were overly generous, and ordinary citizens lacked the funds to purchase lots.

The economic recession, or "panic" as it was called, that began in 1893 was especially severe in the Pacific Northwest, and its impact was felt throughout the decade. Students had a hard time paying tuition, and the school frequently lacked the money to pay faculty salaries. It became common practice to pay faculty, including Chancellor Thoburn, in University Place lots, rather than in cash. Others to whom the university owed money were also paid in lots. For example, two lots to a local printer for printing services rendered, and $950 in lots to Mr. Ouimette in payment of back rent due on the Ouimette Building in downtown Tacoma, where the university was temporarily located.

Then, to make matters significantly worse, in 1898 the Methodist Episcopal Church directed that Puget Sound University merge with Portland University in the hope of creating from two of its financially weak colleges one strong one. In August PSU trustees formally complied with the directive by approving a resolution to merge the two schools. But the sentiment of trustees was not in favor of the merger, and their resolution to merge contained stipulations they felt Portland University could not meet, and they were right.

Portland was to be the merged institutions' location. Chancellor Thoburn, along with those faculty and students he could convince to accompany him, went to Portland in October 1898 and began offering classes with Portland University. But Puget Sound's trustees, who by this time included future president Edward H. Todd, never agreed that the merger had occurred. Their conditions for merging stipulated that "the trustees of [Portland University] should pay the outstanding debts of the Puget Sound University, and give to the purchasers of lots on the site of the Puget Sound University [i.e., University Place], lots of equal value upon the site of the consolidated university." These conditions were to be met by June 1, 1899. When the conditions were not met, Charles McCabe—a member of the church commission that originally came up with the merger scheme—wrote on June 24, 1899, a letter declaring "the decision by which Puget Sound University was consolidated with Portland University to be null and void" and further stating that "there is no legal barrier in the way of re-establishment of the Puget Sound University."

Puget Sound University had been considerably weakened by the merger scheme, both academically and fiscally. Rumors of the merger had circulated well before PSU trustees had even received formal communication about it from the church, causing concern among creditors and donors. This was not what the school needed right then, with sales of University Place lots well below expectations and heavy reliance on donations from local Methodist churches and their members.

The "almost" merger with Portland University was declared by trustees in their September 1899 report to the church to be "the most serious problem of its [the school's] existence." The church, chagrined perhaps at what it had wrought, agreed to support efforts "to rehabilitate the institution."

Yet hopes for University Place were still alive, at least in the minds and hearts of students. The July 1899 *Ye Recorde* declared that upon architect Bullard's return from Pullman, "work will be begun upon the foundation of the first building at University Place."

But by then PSU trustees had lost faith there would ever be a campus at University Place and, increasingly, they wished to get out from under responsibility for the University Land Company. The land company had made promises on behalf of the university to purchasers of lots at University Place, and these purchasers were voicing dissatisfaction with the continued failure to construct a college campus there.

A proposal by the land company to raise $100,000 by selling stock was approved by PSU trustees but went nowhere, and it was probably a good thing it did not.

It was bad enough that over the years some $30,000 from the land company's trust fund to build the campus had been "borrowed" by PSU to pay ongoing operational expenses and to cover the cost of lots deeded to faculty in lieu of salary. Legally, this money had to be repaid, but there was no prospect of doing so. In 1901 the board proposed that the land company accept the university's 95 percent of stock and cancel the $30,000 debt. The land company could then do whatever it wished by way of continuing to sell lots and building a college campus at University Place "for Puget Sound University or some other Christian college."

The university was apparently able finally to get out from under the University Land Company when Pacific Trust Company was incorporated to take over all of the land company's (and the university's) interests at University Place. Pacific Trust also took over responsibility for addressing concerns of lot purchasers, although university officers continued to hear from disgruntled University Place land purchasers for years.

Trustee Joseph Williams (who later became president) wrote in a report that summarizes the university's experience at University Place: "The University Land Company had failed to do what it was organized to do. ... Some have charged us with dishonesty because we have been unable to do as we had hoped. ... Ours was not the only venture that failed during those years. Scores and hundreds of concerns east and west, some of them of great magnitude and of long and respected standing in the business world went down no more honestly than we, and men said no ill of them."

As a result of the Panic of 1893, most of Tacoma's banks had failed, and the Northern Pacific Railroad—the company most responsible for Tacoma's economic and social development—went bankrupt. For Puget Sound University there remained niggling entanglements and obligations stemming from land company activity. The trustees had made good progress on reducing debt, but these entanglements were unending, it seemed. To get out from under them Puget Sound University came to a corporate end in 1903, and the University of Puget Sound was created to carry forward PSU's educational mission.

Today, University Place is a residential suburb of Tacoma located along the west side of a peninsula, with Point Defiance at its tip. It was incorporated in 1995 and has a population of 32,000.

As it was originally conceived, University Place was a good idea at a bad time in the economic life of the country in general and the Pacific Northwest and Puget Sound University in particular. When thinking about all of this, how are we to balance in our minds the enticing, entirely unknowable University Place campus that might have been, against the campus that we actually do have today? The University Place campus might have been magnificent. But so is the campus we have now, and it is real, not a dream. The University Place effort was just one step—albeit a very difficult one—on our path to the heights.

University Place

BIRDS-EYE VIEW OF CAMPUS AS PROPOSED.

WASHINGTON BUILDING.
OFFICES OF
University Land Company.

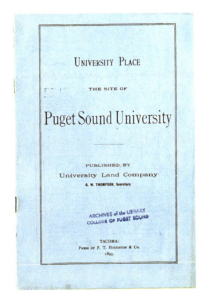

Places of Puget Sound

MAIN BUILDING.

YOUNG LADIES' HALL.

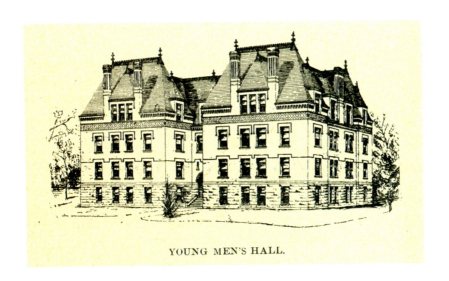

YOUNG MEN'S HALL.

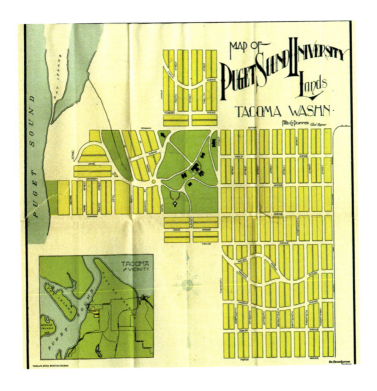

Places of Puget Sound

29. Vienna 1966 and 50 Years of Study Abroad

On February 2, 1966, President R. Franklin Thompson and religion professor and honors program director Robert Albertson '44 drove to Sea-Tac Airport to witness a significant event in the life of the university. Forty juniors and seniors, along with history/foreign language Professor Warren Tomlinson and philosophy Professor John Magee, boarded Pan American World Airways Boeing 707 jet clipper *Viking* to inaugurate the semester study-abroad program. Among the 40 were newlyweds Karen Peterson Finney '67, P'94 and me. Pan Am prepared a large welcome banner that we held for photographs before boarding the airplane. My mother mailed a bon voyage card addressed to us at the airport. The *Viking* took us the polar route to London. Our ultimate destination: Vienna, Austria.

After spending a week in London, a week in Paris, and a week in Rome, our group arrived in Vienna on February 24. We took up residence in the Pension Andreas on Schlösselgasse near the center of the city. Maid service was an improvement over normal college dorm life. Giggly girls cleaned our rooms every day, we never knew when. Karen and I were assigned room 25 on "the girls' side" of the third floor. Room 25 looked onto an inner shaft filled with live and dead pigeons and decades of their droppings. Although the Pension Andreas was less than impressive, and the food was—well, at times pretty terrible, we were located in the heart of Vienna, within walking distance of all the famous places. Bright red trolleys carried us into the hinterlands.

Professors Tomlinson and Magee taught our degree-credit courses. We had regular class sessions in the Pension Andreas, just as if we were on campus, except that we also ate our meals in "the classroom." Professor Tomlinson taught German and History 412, Recent History of Europe. Professor Magee supervised independent study and taught Philosophy 307, Contemporary Philosophy. A local woman taught elementary German. There was only one typewriter in the whole pension so we mostly wrote our papers longhand. Classes were taught in the morning, leaving the afternoons free for study and exploration.

Several of us registered as students at the University of Vienna. Some attended holocaust survivor Viktor Frankl's class on logotherapy, called by some the third Viennese school of psychotherapy. Frankl autographed our copies of his book *Man's Search for Meaning*.

Professor Magee brought with him to Vienna his wife, Kathryn, and his daughters, Mary and Kathy. John and Kathryn lived in their own apartment, while the girls attended an American school with classes in English and boarded at an establishment where only German was spoken. The Magees had a housewarming on March 12, and we students gave them a frying pan and a coffee pot. One weekend Professor Magee disappeared and returned from Munich with a brand new ruby-red Volkswagen 1600 squareback that cost $1,700.

Professor Tomlinson lived with us at the pension. He was in charge and he was our mom and dad. He regularly set up shop at his "money table" and dispensed allowances for the five meals we ate outside the pension each week—dinner on Thursdays and lunch and dinner on Saturdays and Sundays. Our food allowance was 20 Austrian schillings, or eighty cents, per meal.

Magee and Tomlinson were superstars on the Puget Sound faculty and it was no wonder they were selected to lead the school's first semester-abroad group. In fact, I consider Warren Tomlinson to be Puget Sound's father of study abroad. His experience as a world traveler was vast and his enthusiasm for travel contagious.

Professor Tomlinson watched out for us, like the time he rescued Cal Peterson and me when we were detained by Russian soldiers after we—as the Cold War raged—stupidly photographed Soviet military maneuvers in Hungary on a bus trip to Budapest. And he worried about us when he had to. When one of our number failed to return from spring vacation on time and he had no idea where this person was, Professor Tomlinson expressed the degree of his worry this way: "I now know what it feels like to be standing naked on a mountain top during a blizzard."

Outside of class there was a lot to do in Vienna. For example, we quickly learned that opera is more than a lady screeching and a man growling at you from a tinny radio. It works this way: You arrive in Vienna an innocent child and you leave loving opera. You can't help it when the stories, the acting, the singing, the music, and the setting are the best in the world. The Vienna State Opera House, or Wiener Staatsoper, was the first Viennese building reconstructed following World War II. Sometimes we got *stehplatz* tickets for twenty-eight cents and stood throughout the performance, as we did on May 6 for Giuseppe Verdi's *Die Macht des Schicksals (The Power of Fate)*. Other times we splurged for actual seats as we did on March 19, spending $2.60 to see Johann Straus' *Die Fledermaus*.

We saw ballet, too. On April 20 a bunch of us stood in line at the opera house for six hours, beginning at 4 a.m., to get tickets for the April 25 performance of *Swan Lake*, choreographed by Rudolf Nureyev and starring him as Prince Siegfried. Those tickets were expensive, $2.88.

One Saturday, 10 of us rented a VW bus and drove three hours to Graz, Austria's second largest city. On the way back we passed through the town of Kindberg, which seemed friendly enough until a policeman informed us it was illegal to carry 10 persons in a VW bus and that one of us would have to get out. One of us did, but rather than taking up permanent residence in Kindberg, he started walking. After the rest of us admired Kindberg's maypole for a while, we picked him up on the way out of town. A few miles down the road we ran out of gas. Although the VW lacked a gas gauge it did have a reserve tank, or so we thought. We never found the reserve tank and a kid on a scooter came to our aid. He fetched us two liters of gasoline and we were on our way.

Most of us were juniors, but we also had five graduating seniors in the group (Russ McCurdy, Rodney Johnson, Victor Nelson, Jim Nelson, and Doug Smith, all Class of 1966). On May 27 we held a genuine University of Puget Sound Commencement ceremony and banquet at Palais Palffy, a palace located in Vienna's inner city. A representative of the U.S. ambassador to Austria attended.

The semester ended and May 31 was our last day at the Pension Andreas. Most of us spent some or all of the summer traveling in Europe. Karen and I financed our travels by cashing in our return airline tickets. Airfare was expensive in 1966 and the $700 we got for our tickets was sufficient to fund several more weeks of travel in Europe, passage (for $145 each) on the student ship *MS Aurelia* from Le Havre to New York, 10 days with relatives in New England, and a rail trip across the country home on New York Central's *New England States* and Northern Pacific's *North Coast Limited* streamliners.

I don't believe any of us thought in spring 1966, when we went to Vienna, that we were making history. But 50 years later, it seems to me that we did, given the success of that first semester-abroad experiment and the degree to which study abroad then came to be an integral component of a Puget Sound education for so many students.

Beginning in 1951 Puget Sound had sponsored summer study-abroad programs for college credit, including several trips to Sweden led by Professor Tomlinson and German Professor/former Registrar Christian Miller. Vienna 1966 demonstrated that *semester* study abroad worked. The university continued to sponsor such programs, in Vienna and Rome and Breukelen (Holland) early on and then in the 1970s in other places, such as London and Dijon (France) and Grenada (Spain) under the umbrella of ILACA (Independent Liberal Arts Colleges Abroad), a consortium of Pacific Northwest independent colleges, including Puget Sound. At the same time our signature yearlong Pacific Rim program began, with travel abroad scheduled once every three years.

Nowadays most study-abroad opportunities fall under the umbrella of national study abroad consortia with which Puget Sound is affiliated, such as IES, the Institute for the International Education of Students; and CIEE, the Council on International Education Exchange. And in most cases students live with host families, not all together in a group, as we did. Study-abroad options today are almost unlimited.

Postscript: For many years the university, through ILACA, co-sponsored two semester-abroad programs in England, one in London and another in Watford. Our daughter, Karen Finney Lippert '94, P'27 (we hope), spent the spring semester of her junior year at Watford. A few years later, when she met her future husband Dave, a 1995 Willamette University alumnus, they had something to talk about when they discovered that he too had been at Watford. They had missed each other by one year.

Jerianne Fopp, Bob Sprenger, Elizabeth (Libby) Brown, and David Johnson prior to departure for London from Seattle-Tacoma International Airport, February 2, 1966. The airplane is Pan Am's jet clipper Viking, *the Boeing 707 that carried students and faculty to London.*

Vienna 1966 semester abroad student Dianne (Dee Dee) Dressel wearing her dirndl in the Volksgarten (People's Garden), Vienna, Austria, May 21, 1966.

Vienna 1966 and 50 Years of Study Abroad

Vienna 1966 semester abroad students and faculty prior to departure for London from Seattle-Tacoma International Airport, February 2, 1966. From left, the three seated on the floor in front are Betty Blanchard, Jerianne Fopp, and Karen Finney. Kneeling on the floor: Anne Alworth, Doug Smith, Al Howe, Charles Curran, Al Nordell, John Johnston, Steven Bradley, Russ McCurdy, John Finney, and Frank Osmanski. The five women on the floor at right are Mary Margaret Hillier, Diane Garland, Jo Baxter, Janet McLellan, and Isa Werny. Standing, from left: Larry Nicholson, Rod Johnson, Cal Peterson, Liz Watson, Jim Nelson, Peter Galloway, Al Campbell, Don Taylor, Gary Birchler, Victor Nelson, Gordon Cooke, Kay Hatfield, Dianne (Dee Dee) Dressel, Bob Sprenger, David Wagner, Elizabeth (Libby) Brown, Jean Crosetto, Warren Tomlinson, Kathryn Magee, Larry Otto, and John Magee. Not in the photo are Georgia Depue, David Johnson, Gerard Kern, Lexi Roberts, and Mary and Kathy Magee.

Places of Puget Sound

Vienna 1966 semester abroad students eat lunch in the Pension Andreas, Vienna, Austria, May 26, 1966. Identifiable students in this photo include John Johnston, Jim Nelson, Karen Finney, Dianne Dressel, Anne Alworth, Betty Blanchard, Diane Garland, Steven Bradley, Jean Crosetto, Gary Birchler, Georgia Depue, Doug Smith, Mary Margaret Hillier, Al Nordell, Lexi Roberts, Al Campbell, Bob Sprenger, David Wagner, Isa Werny, Janet McLellan, and Gordon Cooke. Professor Warren Tomlinson sits at his "money table" just right of the chalk board.

Vienna 1966 semester abroad professor Warren Tomlinson dispenses cash for food at his "money table" in the classroom/dining room of the Pension Andreas, Vienna, Austria, May 26, 1966.

Personal Stories

30. The Methodist Connection

If someone asks me, "When, exactly, did you first come to Puget Sound?" I respond in one or another of these three ways: (1) 1976, when I started working at the college, (2) 1963, when I enrolled as a freshman on campus, or (3) 1944, when I was born. The Methodist connection, you know.

Puget Sound was established in 1888 by the Methodist Episcopal Church to educate Methodists and to prepare prospective preachers for seminary. From the beginning the college and the church were connected. The Methodist connection linked the two institutions and was in the early days a major factor in the decision of many students, faculty, and staff to attend or teach or work at Puget Sound. But gradually, over a long span of time, the Methodist connection became less important in college choice or career decisions. The connection was severed, at least formally, when the college became independent of the church in 1980. But the Methodist connection lingers at this place, and sometimes reaches out to grab you when you least expect it. This happened to me again recently.

But first, some personal history. My father was a Methodist minister and that made me a preacher's kid, or PK, as we were called. My dad and John Magee were in the same Boston University School of Sacred Theology graduating class, 1941. They joined the Pacific Northwest Conference of the Methodist Church at the same time, in June 1941. After earning a doctorate at Harvard, John Magee joined the Puget Sound faculty and became one of the brightest stars in our teaching firmament. My dad went the pastoral ministry route. He and my mom spent their working lives serving Methodist churches, including two in Seattle during the 1940s—Woodland Park and Grace. I came along at Woodland Park, in 1944.

Because of the Methodist connection, my dad drove to Tacoma often to the College of Puget Sound, where Methodist preachers and parishioners congregated during their annual conferences and at other times during the year. Summers, the college put on weeklong ministerial training and refresher courses, and my dad attended some of those. Sometimes I accompanied my dad on those trips to Tacoma. My visits to Puget Sound were a routine part of being a PK. Puget Sound became "my" school, because of the Methodist connection.

The Methodist connection played a role in my decision on where to go to college. My mother, an Easterner, recommended Bowdoin. I applied to several colleges, but in the end my choice was UPS. It was "my" school, after all. And in those days PKs received 50 percent tuition remission, cutting the annual tuition bill from $850 to $425.

After graduating I left Puget Sound for a while—graduate school and first job and all that. But after nine years I came back, like I always wanted to, and worked at the college 31 years. Thomas Wolfe said you can't go home again, but sometimes you can, if the connection is strong enough. The Methodist connection was strong enough.

Now I am an old guy, volunteering in the university archives, having fun. I am currently immersed in what we in the archives know as Record Group 04.03, the John Blake collection of some

4,500 large format, 4x5-inch, black-and-white negatives. Former publicity director Blake's collection of images from mid-20th century is, not surprisingly, full of Methodists. I am used to that by now. That no longer yanks my Methodist connection chain.

But the other day I came to image 2271. It shows a bunch of Methodist preachers and laypeople sitting in Jones Hall auditorium at 3 p.m. on a lazy June afternoon in 1951. The church's June annual conference week consists mostly of meetings—lots of them. My dad always attended all of the meetings he was supposed to attend—he never skipped, as some of his preacher pals did.

As I scrutinized image 2271 (shown below), the Methodist connection reached out and grabbed me, hard. Four seats in, second row, is a young man with dark hair, paying careful attention to what Bishop Gerald Kennedy is saying, not gazing around or napping or day-dreaming like some. My dad. He was 36. The Methodist connection lingers at this place.

Personal Stories

31. My Life as a Cold War Spy

My wife Karen and I received our bachelor's degrees in 1967, but before that, during spring 1966, the spring semester of our junior year, we studied abroad with 38 other Puget Sound students in Vienna, Austria. We brought along with us our own professors—John Magee and Warren Tomlinson, both superstars among Puget Sound faculty. We took our degree courses from Magee and Tomlinson right where we lived at the Pension Andreas—a kind of urban slum building—in Vienna. In addition, we sat in on courses at the University of Vienna and were registered there as students.

Sometimes on weekends we would tour around to various destinations, either in groups of students or by ourselves. On one occasion Karen and I and 14 other Puget Sound students accompanied Professor Tomlinson on a bus trip from Vienna to Budapest, Hungary. The Cold War between the West and Soviet Bloc countries was raging at the time, and the border between Austria and Hungary was part of the so-called Iron Curtain separating the two sides. Vienna, located in eastern Austria, is only about 50 miles from the Hungarian border, and about 150 miles from Budapest. We thought it was mighty exciting to venture into Hungary, a country under Soviet domination. We had, after all, spent our childhoods diving under school desks so the Soviets' atom bombs wouldn't fry us.

At 7 a.m. on Saturday, May 14, we set off for Hungary. The Hungarian border, near Mosonmagyaróvár, consisted of an unfriendly looking fence with tall guard towers and a no man's land beyond. About 60 miles down the road toward Budapest our bus stopped in the small town of Tata, Hungary, so we could rest and stroll around a bit.

When we got off the bus, we spotted a convoy of military vehicles in the town. Soviet army trucks were rolling down the street and others were stopped by the side of the road, with soldiers milling about. This was cool, and I aimed my camera right at the convoy and took a photograph. I was excited by the fact that my camera had captured the image of a soldier, who was clearly an officer, striding right toward me. I was a little nervous, but he just passed me by and didn't say a word.

A few minutes later a nervous young Russian soldier approached me. He knew a little German and so did I, so that's the language he used to try to get across to me that I was to come with him to the *polizei* station, because I wasn't supposed to be taking any pictures and my film would be confiscated. The soldier was polite, but he had been ordered by the officer I had photographed to haul me in. So Karen and I went with him to a desolate, barren building, where upstairs we found Cal Peterson '67, another member of our student group. Cal had also been hauled in for taking pictures of the soldiers and their vehicles. Quite a few of the other students from our group were there with us for moral support, and soon Professor Tomlinson arrived to find out what was going on.

When Cal Peterson was taken into the office of the local police chief for interrogation, Professor Tomlinson demanded to go in, too. Poor Cal Peterson was lucky to have Professor Tomlinson with him that day. Professor Tomlinson had a Ph.D. from the University of Berlin and taught history, German, and political science courses. He was a world traveler and knew precisely what was going on in that little Hungarian town. He was Cal Peterson's salvation and mine, too, and he never said to either of us, "You idiots!"

After an hour of ins and outs and runnings around on the part of various soldiers and police in their dealings with Cal Peterson and Professor Tomlinson, it became obvious that the officials had forgotten about me. During a lull in the negotiations Professor Tomlinson sidled up to me and murmured, "Why don't you slip on back to the bus, while I stay with Cal?" When the police chief demanded that Cal Peterson be detained, I merged into the middle of the pack of students who returned to the waiting bus. The heat was off me. And I still had my film. We continued toward Budapest.

But Professor Tomlinson was not on the bus with us, nor was Cal Peterson. They were taken two and a half miles down the road to the town of Tatabanya, where Cal's film was confiscated and supposedly developed. In the history of photography there were few films more difficult to develop than Kodachrome. It was a very exacting process. Did Tatabanya, Hungary, have a Kodachrome color processing facility? Maybe, but I doubted it. In any case, Cal lost his film, but he and Professor Tomlinson were finally released. Professor Tomlinson demanded they be taken on to Budapest but was refused. He then demanded that their train fare to Budapest be paid, but they were again refused. They paid their own train fare. We on the bus arrived in Budapest at 2 p.m., but Professor Tomlinson and Cal Peterson did not arrive until much later. We were greatly relieved to see them.

When Professor Tomlinson and Cal Peterson described their experience, the Hungarian officials who hosted us in Budapest were outraged by the treatment we had received at the hands of small-town officials. We learned that the people of Hungary did not like being dominated and controlled by the Soviet Union or the Hungarian government the Soviets had installed. Only 10 years earlier, in 1956, the people had engaged in a spontaneous revolution in which 2,500 Hungarians died before the revolt was suppressed. In Budapest we saw the bullet holes in the buildings.

To us young students from the University of Puget Sound, the Hungarian revolution was ancient history, but in fact it was still going on in the course of world events. And we were right smack in the middle of it and the Cold War. I wrote in my journal that day: "The affair points up the tension between the Russian authorities in this area and the Hungarian officials themselves. Formal complaints are being made all over the place, and the matter is not closed. One poor, bungling, small-town police chief is in for it, as the whole tide of Hungarian receptivity and warmth toward Western visitors is against this small-town autocracy."

The Hungarian people were wonderful, as were the lower-rank Russian soldiers we met. This kind of experience and understanding is why students do and should study abroad. In Budapest the food was wonderful and the hospitality gracious. We saw much of the city and returned to Vienna the next day after an enjoyable overnight stay. My life as a "cold war" spy had been brief, but exciting. I decided I wouldn't take any more pictures of the Red Army. But I treasure the one I have, the one I took in Tata, Hungary, that day in May 1966.

The Iron Curtain between Hungary and Austria, near Mosonmagyarovar, Hungary, May 14, 1966.

The Soviet army officer at right had the Cold War spy hauled in for taking this picture in Tata, Hungary, May 14, 1966.

Personal Stories

Downtown Budapest in 1966 was a much quieter scene than it is today.

Puget Sound Historical Record

Presidents, Academic Deans, Bursars, Registrars, and Deans of Women

Prior to 1913 the president did pretty much everything administrative himself, although faculty frequently performed dean or student record-keeping duties. The separate offices of the president, dean, bursar, registrar, and dean of women developed after 1913 during Edward H. Todd's presidency as part of his rationalization of administration and "getting the house in order." These were, until 1948, the five top administrative officers of the college. Many who held these positions were long-serving.

PRESIDENTS

1890-1892	Fletcher B. Cherington
1892-1898	Crawford R. Thoburn
1898-1900	Wilmot Whitfield
1900-1903	Charles O. Boyer
1903-1904	Edwin M. Randall
1904-1907	Joseph E. Williams
1907-1909	Lee L. Benbow, (acting president 1907-1908)
1909-1913	Julius C. Zeller
1913-1942	Edward H. Todd
1942-1973	R. Franklin Thompson
1973-1992	Philip M. Phibbs
1992-2003	Susan R. Pierce
2003-2016	Ronald R. Thomas
2016-	Isiaah Crawford

ACADEMIC DEANS/ACADEMIC VICE PRESIDENTS
(chief academic officers)

1913-1918	Arthur L. Marsh
1920-1922	Albert B. Cunningham
1922-1926	George F. Henry
1926-1931	Allan C. Lemon
1931-1936	Raymond G. Drewry

1936-1960	John D. Regester
1960-1965	Norman Thomas
1965-1969	Robert H. Bock
1969-1970	Thomas Sinclair (acting dean)
1970-1972	J. Maxson Reeves (died in office on October 4, 1972)
1972-1973	E. Delmar Gibbs (acting dean)
1973-1994	Thomas A. Davis
1994-1996	David B. Potts
1997-2004	Terry A. Cooney
2004-	Kristine M. Bartanen

BURSARS/FINANCIAL VICE PRESIDENTS
(chief financial officers)

1916-1946	Charles A. Robbins
1946-1971	W. Gerard Banks
1971-1979	Lloyd Stuckey
1979-1996	Ray Bell
1996-2000	Mike Rothman
2001-2004	Karen Goldstein
2004-	Sherry Mondou

REGISTRARS

1913-1918	Arthur L. Marsh (dean and registrar)
1919-1926	Charles A. Robbins (registrar and bursar)
1926-1931	Allan C. Lemon (dean and registrar)
1932-1946	Christian Miller
1946-1959	Richard Dale Smith '36
1950-1952	Dean of men and professor of education Raymond Powell served as interim registrar 1950-1952 during Richard Dale Smith's Korean War service as a Navy lieutenant commander, third in command on the aircraft carrier *Essex*
1959-1968	Jack McGee
1968-1976	Olivia Arnason
1976-2007	John Finney '67
2007-2017	Brad Tomhave

DEANS OF WOMEN

1922-1923	Eleanor Brooks Gulick
1923-1924	Elenora Wesner
1924-1925	Valliere Fryer
1925-1927	Louisa McIntosh

1927-1930	Blanche Stevens
1930-1931	Edna Warren Cheney
1931-1953	Lyle Ford Drushel
1953-1956	Leona Murray
1956-1958	Frances Swayze
1958-1961	Margaret Walker
1961-1972	Mary Curran

TRUSTEE CHAIRS

1889-1895	W.D. Tyler
1895-1898	Ira A. Town (judge and mayor of Tacoma)
1898-1899	J.P. Marlatt
1899-1900	Wilmot Whitfield
1900-1902	Joseph E. Williams
1902-1903	David G. LeSourd
1903-1904	D.L. Rader
1904-1909	J.P. Marlatt
1909-1946	Edward L. Blaine
1946-1964	William Washington Kilworth
1964-1967	Roe E. Shaub
1967-1986	Norton Clapp
1986-1993	Lowry Wyatt
1993-2004	William T. Weyerhaeuser
2004-2010	Deanna Watson Oppenheimer
2010-2016	Richard M. Brooks
2016-	Robert Pohlad

STUDENT BODY PRESIDENTS

1905-1906	Earle V. Sheafe
1906-1907	Raymond E. Cook
1907-1908	Gilbert Q. LeSourd
1908-1909	Alta Hathaway
1909-1910	Ernest Mathews
1910-1911	G. Tolbert Crockett
1911-1912	Berna L. Miller
1912-1913	Mamie Conmey
1913-1914	Jack Murbach
1919-1920	Clyde Kinch
1920-1921	Ernest Clay
1921-1922	Anton Erp
1922-1923	Alfred Matthews

1923-1924	J. Everett Buckley
1924-1925	Chester Biesen
1925-1926	Eldon Chuinard
1926-1927	Harold Huseby
1927-1928	Torrey Smith
1928-1929	C. Amos Booth
1929-1930	Charles M. Anderson
1930-1931	Louis O. Grant
1931-1932	Wilbur Goss
1932-1933	J. Herman Mattson
1933-1934	William Leveque
1934-1935	Arthur Linn
1935-1936	Charles Zittel
1936-1937	Maurice Webster and Dorothy Belle Hariss
1937-1938	Gordon Tuell
1938-1939	James Docherty
1939-1940	Richard Sloat
1940-1941	Lyall Jamieson
1941-1942	James Paulson
1942-1943	Paul Heuston
1943-1944	Jane Thompson
1944-1945	Leroy Vaughn
1945-1946	Ruth Ann Dodsworth
1946-1947	Philip Garland
1947-1948	Jerry Baker
1948-1949	Clayton Anderson
1949-1950	William Stivers
1950-1951	James Ernst
1951-1952	Calvin Frazier
1952-1953	George Fossen
1953-1954	Warren Hunt
1954-1955	Jim Nelson
1955-1956	Chuck Arnold
1956-1957	Juris Macs
1957-1958	Spence Stokes
1958-1959	Bob McGill
1959-1960	Richard Waterman
1960-1961	Larry Stenberg
1961-1962	Tom Jobe
1962-1963	Tom Crum
1963-1964	Fred Golladay

1964-1965	William Ramseyer
1965-1966	Roy Kimbel
1966-1967	Bill Brown
1967-1968	Clay Loges
1968-1969	Dean Henry
1969-1970	John O'Melveny
1970-1971	Tom Leavitt
1971-1972	Darrel Johnson
1972-1973	David Wissman
1973-1974	Randy Foster
1974-1975	Mike Purdy
1975-1976	Lyle Gelbach
1976-1977	Chris Carletti
1977-1978	Fred Grimm
1978-1979	Scott Jackson
1979-1980	Tom Cummings
1980-1981	Carl Perkins
1981-1982	Aaron Petersen
1982-1983	Mike Healy
1983-1984	John Pilcher
1984-1985	Dan Holsenback
1985-1986	Mike Brown
1986-1987	Steve Emery
1987-1988	Gillian Gawne
1988-1989	Lynn Hendricks
1989-1990	Arden Maynard
1990-1991	Bill Potter
1991-1992	Herman Westreich
1992-1993	Zach Goldberg
1993-1994	Jason Werts
1994-1995	Andy S. Aweida
1995-1996	Jeremy Soine
1996-1997	Brett Kiehl
1997-1998	Kevin Barhydt
1998-1999	Rafael Gomez
1999-2000	Dave L. Bowe
2000-2001	Ryan Mello
2001-2002	David Bahar
2002-2003	Ben Shelton
2003-2004	Darrel Frost
2004-2005	Ryan Cunningham

2005-2006	Alex Israel
2006-2007	Wan Lang Pham
2007-2008	Hart Edmonson
2008-2009	Yusuf Word
2009-2010	James Luu
2010-2011	Dan Miller
2011-2012	Marcus Luther
2012-2013	Brian Ernst
2013-2014	Eric Hopfenbeck
2014-2015	Paige Maney
2015-2016	Nakisha Renee Jones
2016-2017	Noah Lumbantobing

NAMES

1888-1903	Puget Sound University
1903-1914	University of Puget Sound
1914-1960	College of Puget Sound
1960-	University of Puget Sound

LOCATIONS (all in Tacoma except 1898-1899)

1890-1891	Block bounded by South I and J streets and South 21st and 23rd streets
1891-1895	Ouimette Building on the corner of Yakima and South 10th streets
1895-1898	Palmer House on the corner of South 9th and G streets
1898-1899	At Portland, Oregon, in connection with Portland University, which also was a struggling Methodist college. Portland University closed in 1900.
1899-1903	Palmer House on the corner of South 9th and G Streets
1903-1924	Sixth and Sprague avenues
1924-	1500 North Warner, the current campus

ANCILLARY CAMPUS LOCATIONS

Seattle Campus 1971-1985

Filling a demand in Seattle for an evening program for persons seeking degrees in business administration, Puget Sound opened its Seattle campus in 1971 in the Prefontaine Building near Third and Yesler. The campus ultimately offered bachelor's and master's degrees and enrolled between 650 and 700 students at its height. The Seattle campus closed at the end of summer 1985.

University of Puget Sound School of Law 1972-1994

The opening of the law school was President R. Franklin Thompson's last major achievement before he retired in 1973. The law school, which enrolled some 900 full- and part-time students, was a major component of his plan to build a comprehensive university for the Puget Sound region. But the university was soon to pursue a different path. Although the early plan was to bring the law school onto the main campus, that never happened. The law school operated first on South Tacoma Way and then in the Norton Clapp Law Center—the renovated Rhodes Department Store building—in downtown Tacoma. In November 1993 the trustees sold the law school to Seattle University. Secrecy surrounding the transaction created a firestorm in the Tacoma community and on the campus. Seattle University operated the law school in Tacoma until 1999, when Sullivan Hall was completed on the Seattle University campus.

McChord Air Force Base, Fort Lewis, Tacoma General Hospital, Bremerton, McNeil Island Penitentiary, Olympia, and The Evergreen State College
Between the 1960s and the 1980s Puget Sound offered degree coursework variously at each of these locations and at other locations as well. These programs, mostly business administration, public administration, and teacher training, existed out of momentum behind President Thompson's comprehensive vision for the university and because they made money to help support main-campus programs. But in January 1983 the trustees agreed with President Philip M. Phibbs that it was in the best long-term interest of the university to phase out these operations so that resources and energies could be focused on main-campus academic programs. All of these ancillary operations were closed by 1988.

HISTORICAL TIMELINE
1884
At the first conference of the Methodist Episcopal Church in this region, Bishop Charles Henry Fowler suggests creating a college within the geographical bounds of the conference.

1886
The conference votes to establish the new college at Port Townsend in response to the city's pledge to provide land and funds.

1887
The conference renews the search for a location after Port Townsend fails to meet the terms of its pledge.

1888
The conference establishes Puget Sound University at Tacoma after the city pledges $22,000 and land. Articles of Incorporation are signed on March 17. The school includes an academy (prep school) and a liberal arts college.

1890
Classes begin for 88 students on September 15 in an elegant new building costing $60,000, built on the downtown block bordered by "I" and "J" streets and South 21st and South 23rd streets.

1891
The first students graduate from the academy. But the college loses its new building for lack of funds to repay the loan. The building is leased, and two years later sold to the City of Tacoma to become the John A. Logan grade school. Later the magnificent building is torn down and McCarver Junior High School is built on the site. The college rents the Ouimette building (later known as the Imperial Apartments), "quarters of a cheaper grade." (See Rev. Joseph E. Williams 1902 document in *Volume of Miscellaneous Manuscripts written by Men who took part in the founding and early History of College of Puget Sound, Volume I*, University Archives Mss 034.) President Cherington provides less than full disclosure in his statement in the 1891-1892 college catalog: "Temporarily, commodious quarters will be occupied in the Ouimette Block, corner Yakima Ave. and 10th St. Until street car lines are extended to the University Building this will be a great convenience to students."

1892
The new president, Crawford Thoburn, in his history of the university in the 1892-1893 catalog, writes: "For the first year college sessions were held in the large and elegant University building on I street, but the location proving somewhat inconvenient, owing to the absence of street car facilities, a removal to the Ouimette building corner Yakima avenue and 10th street, was effected at the commencement of the last academic year. This arrangement will continue in force for two years more, when the original location will be re-occupied." It never happened, as hopes for saving the building faded and the lease of the building turned into the sale of the building.

1893
The first students, four in number, graduate from the College of Liberal Arts. A deep economic recession severely constrains the college's ability to borrow or raise funds. Eighteen of 21 Tacoma banks fail.

1894
Land in what is later known as University Place becomes available "at reasonable rates and on easy terms." University trustees envision there "a delightful college community and residential suburb of Tacoma" (both quotes *Williams*, 1902). In an effort to raise funds for building, they create the University Land Company to sell lots around the proposed campus. This venture fails, and the meager proceeds from the sale of lots are instead used to help pay the college's operational expenses. Finally, in 1949 lots 1, 2, and

3, Block 102, Second Division, University Place, that the college had held onto for 55 years, are sold and the proceeds are put into endowment. This sale represents an unusual bridge of sorts between the two corporate entities, the old Puget Sound University and the modern College of Puget Sound.

1894-1895
At the end of the academic year Browder Brown is the first College of Liberal Arts graduate to complete all four years of the Puget Sound University curriculum. Classes are taught in both the Ouimette Building and in Palmer House, so called because it is the former Palmer Hotel, located at South 9th and "G" streets.

1895-1896
Classes are taught at Palmer House through 1903, with the exception of 1898-1899.

1898-1899
Fall semester classes are taught at Portland, Oregon, in cooperation with Portland University, another small, struggling Methodist college. Some hope this will lead to permanent integration as a solution to the financial problems of both schools. But it is clear by December that the consolidation effort is a failure. The university returns in March 1899 to its South 9th and "G" street Tacoma location, greatly weakened in the interval, both academically and financially. President Thoburn dies in May.

1900-1903
For the last three academic years of its corporate existence, Puget Sound University is in such dire financial straits that it is turned over to Dean Orman C. Palmer and Professor Charles Boyer (who serves as president). They become responsible for paying the bills. Anything left over they get to keep. As strange as this arrangement appears, Palmer and Boyer keep the school alive.

1903
The Alumni Association sells the building at South 9th and "G" streets that it has been leasing to Puget Sound University. With no place to hold classes and no money, Puget Sound University comes to its corporate end. The annual conference of the Methodist Episcopal Church creates a new entity, the University of Puget Sound. The Alumni Association purchases land at Sixth and Sprague avenues, where a building is constructed and classes begin in the fall.

1905
Methodist Bishop W.F. McDowell appoints Edward Howard Todd to the post of corresponding secretary of the University of Puget Sound.

1909
Todd resigns as corresponding secretary as a muted protest against the level of debt President Lee Benbow is accumulating for the university.

1913
Edward Todd is sent for and becomes Puget Sound's ninth president.

1914
The University of Puget Sound changes its name to the College of Puget Sound. This is in response to criticism, particularly from the State Board of Education, that the school is less than truthful calling itself a university (in those days the perceived distinction between a college and a university was different than it is now). The board removes accreditation from the school's teacher training program, but quickly reinstates it when UPS becomes CPS.

1915
The college meets the James J. Hill $250,000 challenge.

1916
President Todd hires Charles A. Robbins as bursar. Robbins serves for 30 years and is acknowledged by Todd as being a tireless, energetic partner with him in bringing about the major developments that occurred on campus during that time.

1918
In October classes are cancelled for some weeks due to the influenza pandemic. Three women students die.

A unit of the War Department's Students' Army Training Corps is established on campus in an effort by the department to keep men enrolled until they are needed for service in the war. The SATC program ends after the signing of the November 11, 1918, armistice.

1919
James Rodenburg Slater joins the biology faculty at age 29 after service in World War I. He is instrumental in founding Puget Sound's museum of natural history, now known as the Slater Museum of Natural History. He endows scholarships for students. He retires in 1951, then continues to be active at Puget Sound almost until his death in 1989 at age 98.

1919-1921
In a furious two-year burst of fund-raising activity, the college raises $1 million in two half-million dollar campaigns for endowment and buildings, as the college prepares to move to a new campus. The first half-million is raised from the citizens of Tacoma and

Pierce County in an effort many believed was doomed to fail. The Methodist Church and its members contribute the second half-million.

1921

Although there is nothing on it except a farm house, the new campus is dedicated on June 8. A large boulder acquired from the city during street grading is engraved with these words and becomes the campus cornerstone: "College of Puget Sound campus, dedicated to the promotion of learning, good government, and the Christian religion, June 8, 1921." The cornerstone resides for some years on Warner Street, north of the Anderson Hall site, then for some decades to the immediate south of Jones Hall. During a period of banishment during the 1990s and early 2000s the campus cornerstone lies face down in the President's Woods, rescued from the dump by concerned buildings and grounds staff. In 2003 the campus cornerstone's face is turned to the heavens once again. The cornerstone rests now at the northeast corner of Kilworth Chapel.

1923

Groundbreaking for the first building on the new campus, Jones Hall, takes place on May 22, benefactor Franke Tobey Jones' 78th birthday. She gives $200,000 (including $180,000 new money and $20,000 of her late husband's previously pledged gift) to build Jones Hall in memory of her husband Charles Hebard Jones, who died the year before. The college sells the old Sixth and Sprague campus to Tacoma Schools for $48,000. College buildings are removed and Jason Lee Junior High School is built, named for a former Methodist missionary.

1924

The Jones Hall cornerstone is laid on February 22. In June, graduation ceremonies for the Class of '24 are held in Jones Hall, still under construction. On the same day, students carry the color post from the old campus to the new. In the fall, Jones Hall officially opens and classes begin on the new campus.

John Dickinson Regester is hired as head of the Department of Philosophy and Psychology. He begins more than four decades of service as professor, dean of the college, and dean of the graduate school. He is the longest-tenured dean (1936-1960) in the school's history.

1925

A chapter of national SPURS, sophomore women's service honorary, is established on campus and for 81 years provides volunteer service at a great many functions across the campus. SPURS is an acronym for Service, Patriotism, Understanding, Responsibility, and Sacrifice. SPURS members with their white sweaters bearing the prominent spur logo appear in hundreds of images in the university archives and in the online A Sound

Past digital image collection. Men are admitted to SPURS beginning in the 1970s. Both the local chapter and the national organization are dissolved in 2006. That same year a local chapter of Phi Eta Sigma National Honor Society is established to continue the function and spirit of SPURS on campus.

1927
The college relaxes its prohibition against dancing and for the first time allows dancing at college functions when these are properly chaperoned.

Warren L. Perry is named college librarian. Perry, highly regarded on campus and in library circles, oversees construction of Collins Memorial Library and serves for 36 years.

The Puget Sound Annual Conference of the Methodist Church states in September 1927 its relationship to the College of Puget Sound: "We desire to record the fixed purpose of this annual conference to maintain the control of our College and so direct its affairs in the social and religious life of our students, that the highest and finest traditions and practices of our Methodism shall be maintained" (quoted in Todd, 1947). This formal relationship, enforced through church election of trustees, is gradually relaxed over the next 53 years. In 1980 the formal relationship is dissolved, and the tie between church and university becomes a historical one.

1930
The first bookstore opens January 30 in Jones Hall. In 1942 the bookstore moves into Kittredge Hall, the new student center, and in 1959 to the new Student Union Building, now Wheelock Student Center.

1931
A cooperative program with Tacoma General Hospital is established that lasts into the 1980s. Students enrolled in the program spend three years at the college and two years at Tacoma General Hospital. At the end of the five years students receive a nurse's certificate from the hospital and a bachelor's degree from the college.

Franke Tobey Jones dies on April 25 at age 85.

1932
Coolidge Otis Chapman is hired as professor of English and enjoys a distinguished career at Puget Sound. Today, honors students may graduate with Coolidge Otis Chapman Honors.

After meetings in the east, President Todd and trustee chair Edward L. Blaine return home via the Panama Canal, "a restful voyage which gave opportunity for relaxation" (Todd, 1947). After years of successful campaigning, the college now has assets of more than $2 million, a comfortable position that is quite different from the college's pre-Todd era.

The college purchases a used Wurlitzer organ for Jones auditorium at a cost of $4,250, far below the $20,000 cost of a new organ.

The first celebration of Founders and Patrons Day is held on February 18 as Leonard Howarth Hall is dedicated.

Because of The Great Depression, the trustees direct that faculty and staff be informed that their salaries are subject to revision at any time during the year. Later this is amended to apply only to those making more than $1,800. No revisions are ever necessary, however.

In November the Association of American Universities places the College of Puget Sound on its approved list. This results in inquiries from far and near for more information about the college.

1934

Professor Hanawalt, who has taught mathematics since 1908, retires and is awarded by the college a pension of $40 per month, with the understanding that he may be called back to help the department if necessary.

The campus bell is dedicated on February 20. At the ceremony is the District Director of the United States Lighthouse service. The bell was cast in 1855, shipped around the Horn of Africa, placed at the entrance to the Strait of Juan de Fuca, then placed at Point No Point and finally at Brown's Point before being given to the college. For some years it rings the noon hour from within its bell house between Jones Hall and the Music Conservatory. The bell is returned to Brown's Point in the 1980s.

1935

On February 19 the trustees authorize establishing a retirement and pension fund for faculty and employees.

1936

The Tacoma Railway and Power Company, which earlier had declined to extend a streetcar line to the college, extends a bus line for a four-month trial period. Patronage is good, and the college has had city bus service ever since.

1938
The college celebrates its 50th anniversary. Anniversary events include the groundbreaking for Anderson Hall for women, the first permanent residence hall on the campus.

1939
The college applies for the second time for a chapter of Phi Beta Kappa.

Anderson Hall opens on February 1.

With war on the horizon, the college hires Betty Muller to teach Japanese. Sixteen Japanese students form a Japanese Club "composed of students loyal to the college and the nation." The students give the college 16 Japanese cherry trees that are planted in a friendship circle in front of Anderson Hall. The trees are later moved to other parts of the campus.

1940
The college is chosen by the Civil Aeronautics Administration for the aeronautical training of pilots. Eighteen men receive civilian pilot training certificates.

1941
As faculty are being drafted to military service, the trustees adopt a policy to re-employ them after the war.

1942
Thirty-six students, U.S. citizens of Japanese ancestry, are removed from their studies and placed in internment camps for the duration of World War II. In 2009 they are awarded bachelor's degrees and several are present at the Commencement ceremony.

After 29 years as president, Edward H. Todd retires on July 31 and becomes president emeritus. R. Franklin Thompson becomes president.

1943-1944
Only 62 of 275 enrolled students are men, 23 percent. But on December 6, 1943, 238 Army Specialized Training Program soldiers arrive, almost doubling the enrollment of the college. Some of the men are housed in the gymnasium (the barn, they call it) and some in Kittredge Hall (the palace). They are greeted warmly and have a huge positive impact on the campus. But in March 1944 the ASTP men are called, sooner than expected, to active duty. Many see action, and 16 are killed during the first three days of the Battle of the Bulge.

1946
The college awards General Jonathan Wainwright, a hero of the defense of the Philippine Islands during World War II, an honorary Doctor of Military Science degree.

The Log Chapter of Intercollegiate Knights, a sophomore men's national honorary service fraternity, is established on campus. Together with SPURS, the sophomore women's service honorary, Intercollegiate Knights performs volunteer service on campus at various college functions into the 1970s.

Tuition for 1946-1947 is $125 per semester.

1947
Tuition for 1947-1948 is $150 per semester.

President Emeritus Edward Todd's history of the college is the 50,000th volume added to the library's collection. But Todd continues to work on and expand the volume until June 1950.

Murray Morgan, noted local historian, is hired to teach writing and becomes one of the most popular professors Puget Sound has ever had. During his five years on the faculty (1947-1952) Morgan serves as advisor to *The Trail* and in that capacity oversees one of the most professional, substantive runs of the student newspaper ever published.

1948
After coaching basketball for three years, John P. Heinrick becomes athletic director and head football coach. Heinrick coaches winning teams and becomes exceedingly popular. The 1952 *Tamanawas* is dedicated to him. In 1964 Heinrick retires from coaching football to concentrate on being athletic director and chair of the physical education department.

At the same time Todd Hall opens, a new administrative position, dean of men, is created. Professor Raymond Powell fills the position.

John Blake is appointed the college's full-time public relations director. Under his purview a professional operation is created, headquartered in the basement of Jones Hall, that creates what is known today in the university archives as the John Blake collection of historical photographic images. In 1950 responsibility for the alumni office is added to Blake's duties. Blake serves until 1953.

A brick bus shelter is erected on the southwest corner of North 15th and Lawrence streets under the giant sequoia tree, courtesy of the Northwest Kiwanis Club. The shelter is removed when Lawrence Street is vacated in 1986 and Rasmussen Rotunda is appended to Wheelock Student Center.

Faculty morale gets a boost when the trustees award unexpected bonuses.

The Associated Students of the College of Puget Sound purchase Deep Creek Lodge on Highway 410 near Cayuse Pass as an addition to the college's recreational facilities.

1949
Memorial Fieldhouse opens to honor the 138 former students who lost their lives in World War II.

In basketball, the Loggers defeat the University of Washington, 48-41.

1950
Geology major Raymond Williams is recalled to service in the marines after surviving eight major engagements in the Pacific during World War II. On September 30 he becomes the first Korean War casualty from the College of Puget Sound, killed in the battle for Seoul. The 1951 *Tamanawas* is dedicated to him.

In January Samuel Perkins, Tacoma businessman and longtime friend of President Emeritus Edward Todd, presents a bronze bust of Todd that resides today in Collins Memorial Library. The bust was cast by professor Kenn Glenn of the CPS art department.

Homer Amundsen of Tacoma's Starlite Athletic Club coaches the new CPS varsity boxing team. Unfortunately, Amundsen is unable to fill the team without bringing in outside amateur fighters. Another difficulty is there are no other college teams to box against. The team disbands in January 1951.

On June 7 the Little Chapel in Jones Hall is dedicated to the memory of Gail Pauline Day '37. Today the Gail Pauline Day Memorial Chapel resides on the second floor of Kilworth Chapel.

1951
As was the case during World War II, enrollment of men is once again suffering because so many are being drafted to fight the Korean War. President Thompson applies for and the college is awarded an Air Force Reserve Officer Training Corps detachment. The AFROTC program is headquartered in Memorial Fieldhouse and begins in the fall with great fanfare. It operates for 38 years before closing in 1989.

When the chemistry program receives "national accreditation" from the American Chemical Society in April, the program joins the University of Washington and Washington State College chemistry programs as the only three chemistry departments in the state to be so recognized.

Former President Edward H. Todd dies at age 88 on May 19, two months and two days after his beloved wife Florence dies at age 88 on March 17. They were married 63 years. Florence Todd is reported to have memorized a new poem every day during her lifetime.

General Douglas MacArthur visits campus on November 14 and gives a brief speech in Memorial Fieldhouse.

1952
Student Dick Carlson opens a watch-repair shop in Howarth Hall spring semester, which he calls the Tick Tock Shop.

1956
President Dwight D. and Mamie Eisenhower visit the campus on October 18 on a stop during his re-election campaign. President Eisenhower's speech in Memorial Fieldhouse attracts 6,000.

1957
Deep Creek Lodge is sold for $6,500 as use of the facility dwindles to numbers that cannot sustain it financially. Today Deep Creek Lodge is the Alta Crystal Resort, just down the hill from Crystal Mountain.

1960
As the baby boomers approach their college years, many campuses anticipate a period of extensive growth. President R. Franklin Thompson envisions a larger institution that embraces the entire Puget Sound region with a variety of ancillary campuses and programs, including graduate programs and a law school. On January 1 the College of Puget Sound is renamed the University of Puget Sound.

1961
On October 27 former Vice President Richard Nixon addresses 3,000 in Memorial Fieldhouse. He says that the free world is subject to communist domination if it does not win the Cold War.

1963
On September 27, President John F. Kennedy visits Tacoma and speaks at a Cheney Stadium convocation co-hosted by University of Puget Sound and Pacific Lutheran University.

1966
The Faculty Senate is created.

1969
Anti-Vietnam War sentiment and student agitation against all manner of authority is at its height and finds expression on college campuses across the country. Although the Puget Sound campus experiences no violent confrontations, feelings run high. The trustees establish a University Council to hear arguments and discuss issues raised on both sides.

1970
Students and faculty receive a greater voice in campus decision making. Students and faculty are appointed to trustee committees and the ASUPS president and Faculty Senate chair become *ex officio* members of the trustees' Executive Committee.

1972
University of Puget Sound School of Law opens in September on South Tacoma Way.

The first Faculty Code is approved by trustees.

President Thompson creates the personnel department to ensure compliance with the Civil Rights Act as amended in January 1972 to include college employees. Dean of Women Mary Louise Curran '36 is the first director. The personnel department becomes the human resources department in 1994.

Dale Bailey '56 becomes the first vice president for university relations.

1973
President R. Franklin Thompson retires and is named honorary chancellor for life. Through 1979 he helps with public relations and fundraising, interviews retired faculty and administrators, and writes much about university history.

Philip M. Phibbs becomes president. He serves for 19 years.

The trustees approve a Student Conduct Code and an ASUPS constitution.

The Pacific Rim program assumes its current form, with a yearlong study abroad experience in Asia every third year.

1974
The Collins Memorial Library addition opens.

1975
President Philip Phibbs, anticipating the coming reduction in college enrollments as baby boomers graduate, outlines a new vision for the university. Rather than becoming a regional comprehensive university, Phibbs argues that the university should: remain small; improve the quality of the academic program; work to narrow the range of abilities of students; and increase the number of four-year students, as opposed to those who transfer from other colleges. His vision of a more selective college with a strong faculty and a strong liberal arts program at its center is embraced by trustees and the university community and is the path still being followed today.

1976
The university creates an institutional research office as decision-making in higher education comes increasingly to rely on data and information. John Finney '67, who also serves as registrar, is the first director.

Physical therapy joins occupational therapy as a health science program offered at Puget Sound.

1977
The Budget Task Force is established by President Phibbs to weigh competing budgetary requests and to make recommendations to the president. The Budget Task Force continues to play a key role in the budget-setting process at Puget Sound.

The student radio station KUPS begins broadcasting in April.

The university's first full-time chaplain, the Rev. K. James Davis, is hired.

1978
The core curriculum adopted by faculty in 1976 goes into effect. A core curriculum, rather than general education distribution requirements, has been at the center of the Puget Sound baccalaureate degree ever since.

The university's first Rhodes Scholar, Bradley Severtson, is named.

1980
Trustees of the university are no longer elected by the United Methodist Church. From this time forward the university maintains a historical affiliation with the church but is governed by an independent board of trustees.

The Norton Clapp Law Center is dedicated in September in downtown Tacoma to house the University of Puget Sound School of Law, a law library, and courtrooms.

1981
A new Student Conduct Code is approved by trustees.

1982
An anonymous donor gives the university $3 million to fund sabbatical fellowships for faculty. Fellowships for junior (untenured tenure-line) faculty come to be known as Martin Nelson Junior Sabbatical Fellowships; and fellowships for senior (tenured) faculty come to be known as John Lantz Senior Sabbatical Fellowships, named for physics Professor Martin Nelson and mathematics Professor John Lantz, respectively.

1984
After 15 years on the 4-1-4 academic calendar, the university returns to a semester calendar, but this time it is early-start, with fall semester ending before Christmas, rather than in late January, as was the case prior to 1969.

1985
The university is awarded a chapter of Phi Beta Kappa. This is the culmination of an effort that began "in 1913 or earlier," according to Edward Todd.

The Prelude and Passages student orientation program is established. Later it becomes Prelude, Passages, and Perspectives.

Professor of Religion Robert Albertson '44 is named Puget Sound's first Washington Professor of the Year by the Council for the Advancement and Support of Education. As of this writing, six more Puget Sound professors have received the honor.

Ending a tradition that began in 1942 with construction of Kittredge Hall as the first student center, sorority chapter rooms move out of Wheelock Student Center.

The Student Conduct Code approved in 1981 is revised to become the University Honor Code.

1986
Elizabeth Cousens '87 is Puget Sound's second Rhodes Scholar.

Rasmussen Rotunda is added to the renovated student center.

1987
The summer science research grant program for students begins with a gift from the Murdock Trust. Since then additional donors and funds have increased the number of summer research stipends for students in the sciences and humanities in what is now a well-established program of student research support.

1988
The university celebrates its centennial on March 17.

1989
Paul Fritts '73 builds and installs the Bethel Schneebeck organ in Kilworth Chapel.

Air Force budgetary constraints cause closure of the university's AFROTC detachment after 38 years.

1991
The University Honor Code becomes the Student Integrity Code.

Faculty add International Studies and Science in Context requirements to the core curriculum.

1992
Philip M. Phibbs retires as president. Susan R. Parr becomes president. She later marries and changes her name to Susan R. Pierce. She serves for 11 years.

1994
The university sells its law school to Seattle University, which operates the law school in Tacoma another five years until Sullivan Hall is built on the Seattle University campus.

1995
The Music Building is extended northward to accommodate a concert hall that replaces and greatly expands the capacity of the former recital hall. The original recital hall was named posthumously in the 1960s for longtime music professor and pianist Leonard Jacobsen. The new concert hall is named the Schneebeck Concert Hall in 2002.

1998
The A-frames and chalets that provided temporary office space and student residential facilities under the madrona trees south of Thompson Hall are removed.

1999
Athletic programs move from NAIA to NCAA Division III affiliation.

While maroon and white have been uninterruptedly the school's colors from the beginning, some athletic teams in the 1970s adopted gold and green uniforms in emulation of the successful Green Bay Packers. After years of confusion, all constituencies return to maroon and white in 1999.

Former President R. Franklin Thompson dies on January 15 at age 90.

2003
Ronald R. Thomas replaces Susan R. Pierce as president. He serves for 13 years.

2011
Weyerhaeuser Hall opens and Commencement Walk is built to connect the north and south ends of the campus.

2013
Commencement Hall opens.

2016
Commencement Hall is renamed Thomas Hall to honor retiring president Ronald R. and Dr. Mary Thomas.

Isiaah Crawford replaces Ronald R. Thomas to become Puget Sound's 14th president.

The Athletics and Aquatics Center opens, connected to a renovated Memorial Fieldhouse. The first Hugh Wallace Memorial Pool, attached to the south end of Warner Gymnasium since 1956, closes and is removed after 60 years of use. The new pool is also named Hugh Wallace Memorial Pool.

BUILDINGS
When Edward Todd retired as college president on July 31, 1942, the first six buildings below comprised the entirety of the College of Puget Sound campus.

1908-1952 Music Conservatory
A farm house built in 1908 from a design published in *Craftsman* magazine is the only structure on the new campus at the time the land is purchased. The house is remodeled in 1924 to become a women's residence through 1929-1930. The house is again remodeled in 1930 to become the Music Conservatory until 1952 when it is torn down to make way for today's Music Building.

1924   Jones Hall
Jones Hall is the college's only academic and administrative building when it opens on the new campus. Jones Hall is built with a $200,000 gift from Franke Tobey Jones in memory of her late husband, Tacoma lumberman Charles Hebard Jones.

1924   Warner Gymnasium
The gymnasium serves as the college's only athletic facility until Memorial Fieldhouse opens in 1949. The gym is known for a while thereafter as the Women's Gym, and eventually as Warner Gym.

1927 Howarth Hall
Although construction begins in 1924, Science Hall is not completed until 1927. In 1932 Science Hall is renamed Leonard Howarth Hall after the president of the St. Paul and Tacoma Lumber Company, who died in 1931. Science Hall was built with borrowed money, and $125,000 from Leonard Howarth's estate was used to repay the loan. Howarth Hall serves as the college's science building until Thompson Hall opens in 1968.

1939 Anderson Hall
Named for Agnes Healy Anderson, Anderson Hall opens in the spring semester as a residence hall for women. At her request, the hall is not named Anderson Hall until October 6, 1940, following her death.

1942 Kittredge Hall
The last building constructed during Edward Todd's presidency, Kittredge Hall opens in January as the college's first student center. When what is now called Wheelock Student Center opens fall 1959, Kittredge Hall is reconfigured to become the home of the art department.

1947-2011 South Hall
Returning war veterans bring a huge surge in enrollment. The government makes war surplus buildings available to colleges that will use them to serve veterans. The college acquires surplus army hospital buildings from Paine Field in Everett, Washington. The wooden buildings are transported to Tacoma and are ready for use in the spring. One wing serves the buildings and grounds department. The other two (and eventually three) wings provide offices and classrooms for occupational therapy, philosophy, history, and English. Eventually occupational therapy, and later physical therapy, consume all of the space. After 64 years of service, "temporary" South Hall is torn down in the summer of 2011 after OT and PT move to the new Weyerhaeuser Hall.

1948 Todd Hall
The second residence hall on campus and the first for men, Todd Hall opens in the spring semester. It is named for Edward Howard Todd, the college's ninth president. At age 84, Todd himself trowels the cornerstone into place in June 1947. Todd Hall is the first of some 31 permanent buildings constructed during the Thompson presidency.

1949 Memorial Fieldhouse
Memorial Fieldhouse is dedicated to the 138 former UPS students killed during World War II. When it first opens for the April 1949 Daffodil Festival flower show, Memorial Fieldhouse is the largest venue in Pierce County. Lloyd Silver '49 is the first field house manager. In addition to housing most of the college's athletic facilities, the field house is,

until the Tacoma Dome opens, the site of choice for such public events as the state high school class B basketball tournaments, circus performances, and high school graduation ceremonies. Tennis and racquetball courts in a new structure called the tennis pavilion are added onto the back of the building in 1978. The Pamplin Fitness Center is added in 1994. Memorial Fieldhouse receives a major facelift and renovation in 2015, and in 2016 the attached Athletics and Aquatics Center opens.

1950   President's Residence
R. Franklin Thompson, his wife Lucille, and their daughters Martha and Mary are the first occupants of the president's residence. They move into their new home on Franklin and Lucille's wedding anniversary, June 30.

1953   Music Building
The Music Building is the first classroom building constructed after Jones and Howarth Halls were built in the 1920s. The north end expands northward in 1995 as the old Jacobsen Recital Hall becomes a larger concert hall, named Schneebeck Concert Hall in 2002 for longtime college supporters Bethel and Edwin Schneebeck.

1954   Collins Memorial Library
Dean John Regester cancels classes on April 8 and students and faculty move books from the old library in the basement of Jones Hall to the just-completed Collins Memorial Library. The new library is named for Everell Stanton Collins, who was instrumental in encouraging Edward Todd to accept the presidency in 1913 and who provided long years of financial support and service as a trustee. In 1974 a new wing of the library opens that, along with books, houses faculty offices and classrooms. When Wyatt Hall opens in 2000, faculty and classrooms move out of the library.

1954   Langdon Hall
When completed in 1954, the women's residence hall that later came to be known as Langdon Hall is thought of as an addition to Anderson Hall. During service as interim pastor at Seattle's Plymouth Congregational Church, President R. Franklin Thompson meets Myrtella C. Langdon, whose interests include her church, the YWCA, and, as a result of meeting Dr. Thompson, the College of Puget Sound. She subsequently provides a gift that helps repay the government loan used to construct the Anderson addition. The addition is renamed Langdon Hall and the combined building becomes Anderson-Langdon Hall.

1956   Hugh Wallace Memorial Pool
The college swimming pool added onto the back of Warner Gym in 1956 is named for Hugh Wallace, philanthropist and former U.S. ambassador to France. Don Duncan, the pool's first manager, serves as swim instructor, varsity swim team coach, and pool

manager for some 30 years. In 2016 the pool is replaced by a new one in the Athletics and Aquatics Center attached to Memorial Fieldhouse.

1957   Regester Hall
Built as the second men's residence hall, Regester houses women during its first year, 1957-1958. When Tenzler Hall (called University Hall beginning in 1982 and then Oppenheimer Hall beginning in 2015) opens in 1958, the women return to "the women's side" of campus. For the next eight years Regester Hall is known as New Hall. In 1966 New Hall is named Regester Hall for retiring John Dickinson Regester. Regester joined the faculty in 1924, became dean of the college in 1936, and dean of the graduate school in 1960.

1957   Harrington Hall
Constructed to the same architectural layout as Regester Hall, Harrington Hall houses 77 independent, non-freshman women when it opens. Harrington Hall is named for Margaret Harrington of Seattle, who, inspired by President Thompson, provides funds to aid in construction. Her daughter, Helen Schiff, gives the college a like amount. Harrington and Schiff Halls, located adjacent to each other on the north side of campus, are named for this mother-daughter pair.

1958   Oppenheimer Hall
Named for Flora B. Tenzler, wife of trustee Herman E. Tenzler, Tenzler Hall opens as a women's residence hall. At Mr. Tenzler's direction, it is built with special amenities that instantly make it the most desirable residence hall on campus. The Tenzlers supported many causes in the region and their name appeared on several other local buildings, including the library in the Proctor District of Tacoma. At their request in order to lower the family's public profile, the Tenzler name is removed in 1982 and Tenzler Hall becomes University Hall. Thirty-three years later University Hall is named Oppenheimer Hall in a June 6, 2015 dedication ceremony. Oppenheimer Hall is named for Deanna '80 and John Oppenheimer '80. Deanna Oppenheimer chaired the board of trustees 2004-2010, and she and John are philanthropists and generous supporters of the university.

1958-1999   Burns Field
Dr. W. B. Burns was a longtime Tacoma dentist who in 1898 played baseball for the New York Giants and was a personal friend of Babe Ruth. Located west of Warner Gymnasium, Burns field was the college's baseball field until Wyatt Hall was built. In 2000 a new baseball diamond west of Memorial Fieldhouse opens called West Field.

1959   Wheelock Student Center
The Student Union Building replaces Kittredge Hall as the college's student center in late 1959. Artist Peggy Strong's Paul Bunyan murals move from Tacoma Union Station

to special niches built for them in the SUB's Great Hall. In 1986 Rasmussen Rotunda is constructed, extending into a vacated block of Lawrence Street. The SUB is renamed Wheelock Student Center in 1995 in connection with a major renovation of the building made possible, in part, by Virginia Wheelock Marshall. The building is named for her parents, Tacoma pioneers Anna Lemon Wheelock and R. Arthur Wheelock. At the same time the Great Hall becomes Marshall Hall. In 2013-2014 the student center is renovated once again with an 18,000-square-foot addition.

1961   Smith Hall
Known as South Dorm its first 11 years, this residence hall on the southeast corner of (what was then called) the women's quadrangle is named Smith Hall in 1972. Ward Smith was a local businessman, banker, realtor, and builder. His wife, Rhea-Houston Smith and his son, C. Mark Smith '61, made the renaming possible in memory of Ward Smith's interest in young people and in the development of the university.

1961   Schiff Hall
Helen Schiff and her mother, Margaret Harrington, were prominent Seattle citizens whose interest in the University of Puget Sound grew from their admiration for the leadership of President R. Franklin Thompson. The residence halls named for Margaret Harrington and Helen Schiff sit adjacent to each other along the north side of campus.

1961   Union Avenue Houses
University-owned houses are constructed for Kappa Sigma, Sigma Nu, Sigma Alpha Epsilon, Sigma Chi, and Phi Delta Theta fraternities, with an underground centralized kitchen that provides food to each house. In 1965 three more Union Avenue houses are built, initially occupied by Theta Chi, Beta Theta Pi, and Phi Gamma Delta fraternities. During these years sororities are housed in residence halls. Union Avenue house occupant groups changed over the years, and currently some are occupied by fraternities, some by sororities, and others by independent living groups.

1964   John S. Baker Memorial Stadium
Seating 3,300, Baker Stadium opens September 1964 at a time when the need for new athletic facilities is critically important as baby boomers arrive at college in increasing numbers. John S. Baker was a Tacoma businessman with a strong interest in students and athletics. His bequest to the college made Baker Stadium possible. (John Baker had done good things for the college before. In 1945 he sold the college 11 acres of land at the south end of the campus for $15,000, two-thirds of which he immediately returned to the college as a cash gift. Memorial Fieldhouse sits on that ground.) In 1971 a wall is added on the south side of Baker Stadium, creating storage space under the seats for the physical plant and athletics departments.

1966 McIntyre Hall
Occupying the north side of Sutton Quadrangle, McIntyre Hall houses the economics, sociology and anthropology, and business administration programs. McIntyre Hall is named for Charles Edwin McIntyre, a public relations officer for Weyerhaeuser. His daughter, Lucy McIntyre Jewett '50, and her husband, George F. Jewett, Jr., made it possible for this academic building to be built in her father's memory.

1967 William W. Kilworth Memorial Chapel
William Washington Kilworth was a trustee of the college for 22 years, 1942-1964. For 18 of those years he chaired the board. In his will he left money and specific instructions for construction of the chapel. Unlike most campus buildings built in a modified Tudor architectural style, Kilworth Chapel is constructed in the American colonial architectural style, as Mr. Kilworth wished.

1968 Thompson Hall
Named for R. Franklin Thompson, president of the college for 31 years, 1942-1973, Thompson Hall provides modern facilities for science instruction and research. It replaces Howarth Hall, which had been the college's science building for 44 years. Thompson Hall also opens a new door to the campus, facing Union Avenue. Theretofore the main entrance was North 15th Street, but after Interstate 5 is built, most people arrive via Union Avenue. Thompson Hall undergoes a major two-year renovation during 2006-2008 and, together with Harned Hall, is a part of the college's Science Center.

1969-1998 A-Frames and Chalets
Five 20' x 40' two-story A-frame buildings are constructed to house students beneath the madrona trees south of the Music Building. Later, a few larger wooden structures called chalets are added. When housing pressures ease, some of the buildings are used as administrative offices. The A-frames and chalets are removed in June 1998.

1970 Seward Hall
This residence hall located east of Regester Hall is built in 1970 and named in 1972 for Raymond Sanford Seward and his wife Olive Brown Seward. Seward Hall is the only campus building named for someone who served his entire career on the faculty and for someone who served her entire career in administrative work. Raymond Sanford was professor of physics, 1923-1955. Olive Brown became President Edward Todd's secretary in 1919, married Raymond Seward in 1932, and, when President Todd retired, continued to serve as President R. Franklin Thompson's secretary until 1946.

1971 Ceramics Building
Prior to construction of the 60x80-foot ceramics building north of Kittredge Hall in summer 1971, the art department's ceramicists were located in the basement of Howarth Hall.

1990 Phibbs Hall
Another residence hall known as New Hall for a time is constructed in 1990 south of and connected to Todd Hall. In 1992 New Hall becomes Phibbs Hall to honor retiring president Philip M. Phibbs and wife Gwen Phibbs. Among the university's 12 residence halls, Anderson-Langdon and Todd-Phibbs are the only connected pairs allowing inside passage from one to the other.

2000 Lowry Wyatt Hall
The opening of Wyatt Hall in early summer coincides with a major remodeling of Collins Memorial Library, as humanities faculty move out of the library into the new academic building. Lowry Wyatt was a community leader and philanthropist who served as a university trustee for 26 years, 1970-1996. He chaired the board 17 of those years, 1976-1993. Wyatt Hall significantly expands the campus and moves its academic center southward.

2002 Trimble Hall
Trimble Hall is the first residence hall consisting solely of single-student rooms arranged in suites that share a bathroom, kitchenette, and living space. This large hall, housing 183 students, is named for Charles Garnet Trimble, who served as a Methodist medical missionary in China and as the college's athletic team physician during the 1930s. His memory is honored in this way through the financial generosity of his son, Robert A. Trimble '37, Hon. '93.

2006 Harned Hall
Named for Joe C. Harned '51, Harned Hall opens in 2006, followed by a two-year renovation of Thompson Hall. Together, Thompson and Harned Halls, which are interconnected, comprise the college's Science Center, completed in 2008.

2009 Facilities Services Complex
The facilitites services department vacates South Hall, the former World War II army surplus building, and moves into new facilities south of Memorial Fieldhouse.

2011 Weyerhaeuser Hall
Weyerhaeuser Hall is named for Bill and Gail Weyerhaeuser, longtime supporters of the university. As the college's center for health sciences, Weyerhaeuser Hall houses the occupational therapy, physical therapy, psychology, and exercise science academic programs in a facility that promotes integration of teaching and learning. With the opening of Weyerhaeuser Hall across 11th Street from Memorial Fieldhouse, the old South Hall wooden army surplus buildings are razed and the campus opens up dramatically as its academic center moves southward once again.

2013   Thomas Hall
The university's 12th residence hall opens fall semester 2013 and is known its first three years as Commencement Hall, built on the sites of the human resources department house (known as Mullins House) and the South Hall army surplus buildings razed in 2011. In 2016 Commencement Hall is renamed Thomas Hall to honor retiring president Ronald R. Thomas and wife Dr. Mary Thomas.

2016   The Athletics and Aquatics Center
The Athletics and Aquatics Center opens, attached to the renovated Memorial Fieldhouse. The original Hugh Wallace Memorial Pool is removed. The new pool is also called Hugh Wallace Memorial Pool.

TRADITIONS
The Hatchett
The tradition of the hatchet begins as an annual rite during which, as a symbol of peace between juniors and seniors, the senior class president gives "the true Loggers' axe," an old hatchet reportedly found by students in 1908, to the junior class president while sophomores try to snatch it away. Gradually the tradition becomes not so much one of giving as of finding. Juniors are required, based on clues, to find the hatchet. Seniors usually make it possible for juniors to find the hatchet and the tradition continues and works this way pretty routinely for some 50 years. But over time seniors make it more and more difficult for juniors. Eventually seniors feel they have triumphed if the juniors cannot find the hatchet at all. This leads to long disappearances of the hatchet. As the absences become longer and more frequent, the original nature of the tradition is lost. The hatchet—when it does finally appear—becomes an item to be put on defiant display. For example, after being clandestinely stolen from its student center display case in 2000, the hatchet was missing for some 12 years. The college has apparently moved on, and the original tradition of the hatchet has morphed into something entirely different.

The Color Post
The Color Post as a tradition came into being in 1917 during Edward Todd's presidency and was at that time unique in the country, as it may still be. The Color Post ceremony takes place twice each year, in the fall during the matriculation ceremony when freshmen enter the college, and in the spring, when graduating seniors enter the alumni society.

Campus Day and the Pull
Campus Day was "a time set aside for the annual general spring campus cleanup," to quote from the 1934 *Tamanawas*. On Campus Day students and, frequently, faculty and administrators as well, helped to clean up and otherwise make improvements to the cam-

pus and the neighborhood. This was especially important during the early days. Work activities were followed in the afternoon by food and games, including the pull. The pull was a tug of war between the freshmen and sophomores, the losers becoming thoroughly hosed down. There have been occasional Campus Days in modern times, although maintenance and beautification of the campus is now pretty thoroughly professionalized.

May Day (Spring Festival)
May Day festivities were once common on campuses across the country. Dances, musical numbers, and the crowning of the May Queen were featured during May Festival, held each May on Sutton Quadrangle through the 1960s. In the early 1950s local high schools were invited to name May Princesses who also participated in Puget Sound's May Day spring festival activities. Departments held open houses for prospective students. May Day has morphed into today's Spring Family Weekend.

ACADEMIC CALENDAR
Through 1968-1969
Traditional semester, with fall term ending in January

1969-1970 through 1983-1984
4-1-4, with two shortened semesters and a one-month interim term (called Winterim) in January

1984-1985 to the present
Early-start semester, with fall term ending before Christmas

GREEK LIFE
During the college's early years, students formed literary societies to promote friendship and social interaction within an academic, literary environment. By 1926 eight local social fraternities and sororities had formed, several tracing their roots to the literary societies. Beginning in the late 1940s the local groups began to affiliate with national organizations. By 1966 there were eight fraternities and seven sororities, all with national affiliations. This number has declined to four fraternities and five sororities today. Some of them can trace their Puget Sound roots more than 100 years into the past.

Sororities

Alpha Phi
1922   Local sorority Lambda Sigma Chi is founded ..

| 1953 | Lambda Sigma Chi becomes the Gamma Zeta chapter of national Alpha Phi and continues to this day. |

Chi Omega
1921	Local sorority Delta Alpha Gamma founded
1953	Delta Alpha Gamma becomes the Epsilon Chapter of national Chi Omega
1982	The chapter becomes inactive.

Delta Delta Delta
1926	Local sorority Alpha Beta Upsilon is founded.
1952	Alpha Beta Upsilon becomes the Phi Zeta chapter of national Delta Delta Delta
1997	The chapter becomes inactive.
2016	The chapter reactivates and continues to this day.

Gamma Phi Beta
| 1961 | Gamma Epsilon chapter of national Gamma Phi Beta is founded and continues to this day. |

Kappa Alpha Theta
| 1963 | Delta Iota chapter of national Kappa Alpha Theta is founded and continues to this day. |

Kappa Kappa Gamma
| 1965 | Puget Sound chapter of national Kappa Kappa Gamma is founded. |
| 2005 | The chapter becomes inactive. |

Pi Beta Phi
1898	The Boyer Literary Society is founded.
1909	The Boyer Literary Society divides into two literary societies, one for men called H.C.S., and one for women called Kappa Sigma Theta; by 1921 Kappa Sigma Theta has become a local social sorority.
1948	Kappa Sigma Theta becomes Washington Gamma chapter of national Pi Beta Phi and continues to this day.

Fraternities

Beta Theta Pi
| 1960 | Local fraternity Beta Zeta Pi is founded. |

1961	Beta Zeta Pi becomes Delta Epsilon chapter of national Beta Theta Pi.
2011	The chapter becomes inactive.
2014	The chapter reactivates and continues to this day.

Kappa Sigma

1898	The Boyer Literary Society is founded.
1909	The Boyer Literary Society divides into two literary societies, one for men called H.C.S., and one for women called Kappa Sigma Theta.
1921	The literary society H.C.S. becomes local social fraternity Sigma Zeta Epsilon, "the Zetes."
1948	Sigma Zeta Epsilon becomes a chapter of national Kappa Sigma.
1999	The chapter becomes inactive.

Phi Gamma Delta

1962	Delta Colony of national Phi Gamma Delta is founded.
1966	Delta Colony becomes Tau Omicron chapter of national Phi Gamma Delta.
1971	The chapter becomes inactive.

Sigma Alpha Epsilon

1947	Local fraternity Pi Tau Omega fis ounded.
1951	Pi Tau Omega becomes the Washington Gamma chapter of national Sigma Alpha Epsilon.
2001	The chapter becomes inactive.
2011	The chapter reactivates and continues to this day.

Sigma Chi

1921	Local fraternity Sigma Mu Chi founded.
1950	Sigma Mu Chi becomes the Delta Phi chapter of national Sigma Chi and continues to this day.

Sigma Nu

1924	Local fraternity Alpha Chi Nu is founded.
1948	Alpha Chi Nu becomes a chapter of national Sigma Nu.
2009	The chapter becomes inactive.

Phi Delta Theta

1905	The Philomathean Literary Society is founded.
1922	Local fraternity Delta Kappa Phi is founded by the men of the Philomathean Literary Society.

1952   Delta Kappa Phi becomes the Washington Delta chapter of national Phi Delta Theta and continues to this day.

Theta Chi
1927   Local fraternity Delta Pi Omicron is founded.
1950   Delta Pi Omicron becomes Gamma Psi chapter of national Theta Chi.
1981   The chapter becomes inactive.

SCHOLASTIC AND SERVICE HONORARY SOCIETIES

Intercollegiate Knights
1922   The Knights of the Log is organized as a local service honorary society for men
1946   The Knights of the Log local group becomes the Log Chapter of the Intercollegiate Knights national organization, founded in 1919. The Log Chapter is currently inactive, as is the national organization.

Mortar Board
1922   Otlah Club is organized on campus for senior women, initiated in the junior year for achievements in scholarship, leadership, and service.
1959   The Otlah Club becomes the Otlah Chapter of the Mortar Board National College Senior Honor Society.
1975   Men become eligible for membership.

Mu Sigma Delta
1931   Mu Sigma Delta is organized as a local scholastic honorary society by faculty who are members of Phi Beta Kappa, with the same membership criteria as Phi Beta Kappa. Mu Sigma Delta functions through the early 1970s.

Phi Beta Kappa
1986   The Delta of Washington chapter of Phi Beta Kappa is awarded to the University of Puget Sound.

Phi Eta Sigma
1922   Ladies of the Splinter is organized as a service honorary society for women in parallel to the Knights of the Log service honorary society for men.
1925   A Puget Sound chapter of the national SPURS is established on campus, and the Ladies of the Splinter group is dissolved. For many years SPURS and Intercollegiate Knights operate side-by-side in service to the campus.
2006   The national organization and the Puget Sound chapter of SPURS are dissolved. A chapter of national Phi Eta Sigma is established on campus for sophomores

who have at least a 3.5 grade average as freshmen. This group is seen as a continuation of the service spirit of SPURS.

Phi Kappa Phi

Phi Kappa Phi's mission is "To recognize and promote academic excellence in all fields of higher education and to engage the community of scholars in service to others." The national Honor Society of Phi Kappa Phi was established in 1897; the Puget Sound chapter, some years later.

MAJOR FUNDRAISING CAMPAIGNS

First Endowment Campaign (The Hill Challenge)
Concluded: 1915
Goal: $250,000
Amount raised: $250,000 ($5.9 million in 2016 dollars)
The First Half-Million Dollar Campaign for Endowment and Buildings
Concluded: 1920
Goal: $500,000
Actual amount raised: $510,000 ($6.1 million in 2016 dollars)

The Second Half-Million Dollar Campaign for Endowment and Buildings
(Includes the Everell S. Collins $100,000 Challenge)
Concluded: 1921
Goal: $500,000
Amount raised: $597,723 ($8.0 million in 2016 dollars)

The Third Half-Million Dollar Campaign for Endowment and Buildings
(Includes the Rockefeller Foundation Challenge and the Leonard Howarth Bequest)
Concluded: 1931
Goal: $500,000
Amount raised: $500,000 ($7.8 million in 2016 dollars)

The Centennial Campaign
Concluded 1988
Goal: $45 million
Amount raised: $47.6 million ($96.3 million in 2016 dollars)

Charting the Future campaign
Concluded: 2000
Goal: $50 million
Actual amount raised: $68.5 million ($95.2 million in 2016 dollars)

One of a Kind [The Campaign for Puget Sound]
Concluded: 2015
Goal: $125 million
Actual amount raised: $131.6 million

Sources

More information about the buildings, places, and people of Puget Sound and about the Puget Sound timeline is to be found in Collins Memorial Library's Archives and Special Collections (ASC). Major works used in the preparation of this volume include the student newspaper *The Trail* and its predecessors, *Ye Recorde* and *The Maroon*; the annual student yearbook *Tamanawas* and its 1913 predecessor *Klahowya*; former president Edward H. Todd's history, *College of Puget Sound: A Dream Realized* (1947) and his memoir, *A Practical Mystic: Memoir of Edward Howard Todd, 1950*; former president R. Franklin Thompson's Historical Materials, in four volumes, including his Interviews of Puget Sound People; and other materials in the University Historical Texts collection. Most of these materials are available and searchable online at the library's Sound Ideas web page at soundideas.pugetsound.edu/ups_archives. Valuable also are descriptions accompanying photographs in Puget Sound's searchable online historical digital image collection, A Sound Past, available at digitalcollections.pugetsound.edu/cdm/landingpage/collection/upsimages.

When sources other than those listed above were used, or where additional comments are offered, they are to be found below:

Anderson-Langdon Hall, pages 1-5
Most residence halls on campus, whether built originally to house men or women, house both men and women today. Anderson Hall is unique in retaining physical evidence of the gender of its first residents. Inscribed in the lintel over the southeast door is the word WOMANHOOD.

Collins Memorial Library, pages 7-10
Everill S. Collins' support for the college went far beyond the library. On page 296 of his memoir, President Todd declares that Collins "ought to be called the financial founder of

Sources

the institution." Descendants of Everill S. Collins continue to support Collins Memorial Library today. Furniture in the library's new study areas was provided through their generosity. For information about sustainable logging methods of today's Collins Companies, see www.collinsco.com. Note that the April 17, 1953 issue of *The Trail*, in which the library's April 14, 1953 groundbreaking is reported, was originally printed mislabeled as the April 17, 1952 issue. This mistake could lead one to conclude erroneously that the groundbreaking took place in 1952 rather than in 1953. In the architect Silas Nelson paragraph the quotes are from R.F. Thompson Historical Materials Volume 1, available online at *Sound Ideas*.

Gail Pauline Day Memorial Chapel, pages 11-15
See also the printed program *Baccalaureate Service and Dedication of Chapel, C.H. Jones Hall, June 7, 1925* in the ASC collection. The story of chaplain Jim Davis' search for Gail Day chapel in Jones Hall came to me in a January 2012 personal interview with him. I am indebted to Gail Pauline Day's nephew, Trustee Emeritus Allan D. Sapp '78, who gave to the archives photographs of his aunt and his parents' wedding in Gail Day Chapel.

Kittredge Hall, pages 29-40
Kittredge was expected by many to be the fifth brick building on campus, but in fact it is a wood frame building with a brick veneer. President Todd explained the use of wood as deriving from Tacoma's reputation as "The Lumber Capitol of the World" and from the college's athletic team, "The Loggers." (See his introduction to the document "Roster of Donors to the Student Union at the College of Puget Sound, 1941," in folder 4-19 in Box 4 of the ASC collection UPS Presidents 1888-1942). Plywood and wood products were donated by the St. Paul and Tacoma Lumber Company, Oregon-Washington Plywood Company, Washington Door Company, Model Lumber Company, Reliance Lumber Company, Buffelen Lumber and Manufacturing Company, Wheeler-Osgood Company, Peterman Manufacturing Company, and other concerns. (See the document "Gifts and Pledges to the Student Union Building," in folder 4-15 in Box 4 of the ASC collection UPS Presidents 1888-1942).

On the south side of Kittredge Hall facing North 15th Street are what appear to be two doors, or at least one door with the other bricked over. Over the years many have wondered when that second door, the one to the east, was removed. The answer is—never; it was never a door. According to architect Earl Dugan of the college's architectural firm Sutton, Whitney, and Dugan, as reported in *The Trail*, what looks like a former door is a second archway that provides artistic balance to the south side of the building. The architects felt that without the second archway the building would look imbalanced.

Memorial Fieldhouse: The Commencement Story, pages 55-57
This story was born primarily from my personal experience as chief faculty marshal 1989-2007, during which time arguments for and against outdoor Commencement were waged and the "outdoors rain or shine" approach was developed. My daughter's 1994 graduation was the last to take place inside Memorial Fieldhouse.

The Music Building, pages 59-63
For a *Trail* story on the prospective new Music Building and some of its dimensions and features, see the May 16, 1952 issue, pp. 5 and 6. A photograph of the wooden Music Conservatory building appears on p. 5 of the same issue. Donald R. Raleigh '40's letter was printed in the Spring 2006 issue of *Arches*: "The building served as the conservatory of music during the years that I attended the College of Puget Sound. It was built in 1908 by my maternal grandfather, Norton Lonstreth Taylor. He was city engineer of Tacoma at that time. I was born in this house since my father was serving in the U.S. Army during World War I. One time, Dr. Sinclaire asked me where I was born, and I told him 'the conservatory of music.' He looked a little taken aback until explanations were forthcoming." Mr. Raleigh enclosed a photo with his letter of the house constructed in 1908 at 1503 North Puget Sound, taken shortly after it was built. The photo may be viewed at A Sound Past.

Puget Sound's Bells and Carillon, pages 65-73
The current location and status of the old campus bell was confirmed in October of 2012 through email and telephone communication with Mavis Steers of the Points Northeast Historical Society. The "carillonic bells" quote is from the home page of the Schulmerich company's website at schulmerichcarillons.com. Read the whole story about Jeff Strong's 13-chimes-at-noon prank in the spring 2006 *Arches* at pugetsound.edu/about/offices-services/office-of-communications/arches/back-issues/arches-archive/spring-2006/chime-and-chime-again. Information about the 2001 carillon is from "Ring Out the Old" in the winter 2002 issue of *Arches*. That the alma mater recommenced daily play May 9, 2016, is personal experience of the author who, with co-conspirator Jeff Strong '76, did the deed. The two of us stood in front of the library at noon that day and heard a student exclaim: "It's the alma mater! I wish they would play it every day." Consider it done, we said to ourselves. Information about the Kilworth Chapel bell is from university chaplain Dave Wright on January 19, 2016, and from the university's website at pugetsound.edu/about/campus-the-northwest/places-spaces/kilworth-memorial-chapel.

Regester Hall, pages 75-78
When the dean of men responsibility split off from the academic dean's duties in 1948, education Professor Raymond Powell became the first incumbent. Not coincidentally, the dean of men position was created the same year the first men's residence hall opened, Todd Hall. The college had housed women on the current campus from the beginning,

Sources

and had a dean of women since 1922. For the history of the dean of women position at Puget Sound, see the chapter on Lyle Ford Drushel in this book.

Seward Hall, pages 79-82
See also R. Franklin Thompson's "Interview with Dr. and Mrs. Raymond Seward," May 19, 1978, in ASC or online at Sound Ideas.

South Hall, pages 83-85
For more about the Mead Bill that made war surplus buildings available to colleges to further the education of war veterans, see: "Surplus Property and Veterans Education," by Ernest V. Hollis. *Peabody Journal of Education*, Vol. 24, No. 4 (January, 1947), pp. 234-239, available at jstor.org/stable/1489047.

Thompson Hall, pages 87-92
For a report of a student interview with President Thompson, see "Dr. Thompson Proves Easy to Interview," by Alexander Mortellaro in *The Trail*, October 3, 1947. For a terrific summary of President Thompson's typical day and duties, see *The Trail*, May 11, 1951. Both are available online at *Sound Ideas*.

Todd Hall, pages 93-96
See also R. Franklin Thompson's "Historic Perspective of Todd Hall," in R.F. Thompson Historic Materials, Vol. 2, online at Sound Ideas.

Warner Gymnasium, pages 97-101
For the May 17, 1924, photograph showing the athletic field being graded by horses, see *Supplement to the Quarterly College of Puget Sound Bulletin*, Vol. XVI, No. 3, July 1924. For more about the original 10 quadrangles envisioned by Todd and Sutton see *Quarterly College of Puget Sound Bulletin*, Vol. XVI, No. 4, October 1924. For Lastincote gym floor information search A Sound Past.

Homer Amundsen and Boxing at Puget Sound, pages 103-107
Websites consulted for this chapter are columbianewsservice.com/2011/03/boxing-diasppears-from-college-sports; en.wikipedia.org/wiki/Harvard_Boxing_Club; en.wikipedia.org/wiki/Boxing_in_the_1950s; boxrec.com/media/index.php/Homer_Amundsen; host.madison.com/wsj/news/local/doug_moe/article_4a56a5e8-012c-580d-bde9-21361d66b3a4.html; en.wikipedia.org/wiki/NCAA_Boxing_Championship; boxing.isport.com/boxing-guides/college-boxing-explained; and en.wikipedia.org/wiki/National_Collegiate_Boxing_Association. Also see: The Tacoma *News Tribune*, September 20, 1950.

Coolidge Otis Chapman, pages 109-116
Documents viewed at ancestry.com tell of: Chapman and his brothers' schooling (1915 New York State Census); Chapman's height and weight (*U.S. World War II Draft Registration Cards*, 1942); his marriage to Helen Hume (1930 U.S. Census), his trans-Atlantic sea voyages (UK, Incoming Passenger Lists, 1878–1960, and New York, Passenger Lists, 1820–1957), and his 1940 salary (1940 U.S. Census). Chapman's master's thesis is in the Cornell University Library Catalog.

The November 2, 1951 issue of *The Trail* tells of Chapman's 1951 book. The 1947 *Trail* interview, "Coolidge Otis Chapman Likes All Phases of Literary Life," appears in the November 21 issue. For a brief biographical sketch of Chapman in connection with an upcoming sabbatical, see the January 23, 1950 *Trail*. Chapman's retirement dinner is reported in *Tacoma News Tribune*, May 31, 1959.

Edward H. Todd, the Man Who Saved Puget Sound, pages 117-122
As a young Methodist minister, Todd was a genuine 1890s pioneer in the Puget Sound and Eastern Washington regions. For insights into the man and for a sense of the effort required to move from place to place in the roadless environment see his memoir *A Practical Mystic: Memoir of Edward Howard Todd*, 1950, available online at Sound Ideas.

Charles Arthur Robbins, pages 123-129
Much of what we know about Charles Robbins' duties as bursar is from Robbins' March 1967 document, *Experiences of Charles A. Robbins at the College of Puget Sound from 1916 to 1946 Inclusive*, in hard copy at ASC. The 1940 U.S. Census, viewed at ancestry.com, is the source of Robbins' 1939 salary. In R. Franklin Thompson's *"Interview with Dr. and Mrs. Raymond Seward,"* May 19, 1978, is reference to the Robbins' welcoming Bertha's parents into their home. Robbins tells his story about listening to the radio in the CPS farmhouse in the October 9, 1931 *Trail*. See the October 11, 1940, *Trail* for Robbins' service to WACUBO. Robbins' honorary degree is reported in *College of Puget Sound Alumnus*, June 1947.

Frances Fullerton Chubb, pages 131-139
Before 1926, art courses were offered in connection with the normal, or teacher training, department, and did not include art history. See *College of Puget Sound Bulletin 1926*, pages 49-50. Frances Chubb's Understanding the Arts course description remained unchanged in college catalogs for more than twenty years. See, for example, *College of Puget Sound Bulletin*, 1949-1950, page 60; 1957-1958, page 32; and 1967-1968/1968-1969. Page 25. A beautiful soapstone sculpture Frances made in the 1940s is in the personal collection of faculty emeritus Bill Colby, who showed me the sculpture at his home on February 24, 2015. Regarding Frances' birthplace, she always gave it as St. Marys, Idaho. Her Idaho birth certificate identifies her birthplace as St. Maries, the pronunciation of which is the same as St. Marys. Information on Chubb family history may be found at

wikitree.com/wiki/Chubb-249, and at ancestry.com (*1849-1905 Minnesota, Territorial and State Censuses*, Alonzo's *U.S. World War I Draft Registration Card*, 1917-1918, *United States Census 1940*, and *U.S. City Directory, 1821-1989*). See *Tamanawas* for the years 1936-1939 for information about Frances' student activities. See R.F. Thompson's "Frances Fullerton Chubb," Thompson Histories, Portraits (1900), University Historical Texts, Book 7 in Archives and Special Collections, also available at soundideas.pugetsound.edu/pugetsoundhistoricaltext/7. Dean John Regester kept enrollment records by class section, currently in A&SC, which made it possible for me to compute *Understanding the Arts* average enrollment during the 1950s. See Enrollment-Class Reports folders in RG 02.01, Box 4, ASC. The Karen Finney report was a personal communication, January 2015. The John Delp quote is from an email message to *Arches* editor Chuck Luce.

Lyle Ford Drushel, pages 141-149

I was privileged, while researching Lyle Ford Drushel, to become acquainted with her grandnephews, William (Bill) S. Lingley, Jr. and Ralph David Simpson III, and her grandnieces, Harriet (Hattie) Lingley Dixon and Lyle Elizabeth (Libet) Lingley Gardner. Their emails describing anecdotes of Lyle's influence on them convey the depth of their admiration and gratitude to her and helped me to understand the influence she had on Puget Sound students as well. In addition, they donated to A&SC Lyle Elizabeth Ford's college scrapbook, *School Girl Days: A Memory Book*, Mss.055 in ASC. This memory book contains photographs, documents, and clippings from her Puget Sound student days, and is the source (along with *The Trail* newspapers and the 1913 yearbook *Klahowya*) of what we know about her life 1907-1912 as a Puget Sound student. The book also contains a copy of her Winfield (Kansas) High School 1907 commencement program.

Morris Ford's (Lyle's father) 1929 obituary indicates he had lived in Tacoma 22 years, identifying the year of their move to Tacoma as 1907. For information about Lyle's brother Morris' history with the Franklin Pierce school district see fpschools.org/about_us/district_history.

It is possible that during the 1909-1910 academic year when Lyle was not enrolled at Puget Sound, she may have given teaching a try with credentials earned during two years of college, and then after a year decided to return to pursue a four-year baccalaureate.

See the 1911-1912 catalogue (published May 1911) listing Lyle Elizabeth Ford as an assistant in English (p.15), and the 1912-1913 catalogue (published June 1912) listing Lyle Ford as instructor in English (p.14). Lyle's service at Astoria during WWI is documented by the Certificate of Service in her memory book.

About Allen Drushel, see *Bulletin of Yale University: Obituary Record of Graduates of Yale University 1930-1931*, pages 167-168, available online at mssa.library.yale.edu/obituary_record/1925_1952/1930-31.pdf. The train theory of Lyle and Allen's meeting is articulated in an email from grandniece Hattie Dixon, April 1, 2015. The backseat of a bus theory is articulated in an email from Lyle's grandnephew William S. Lingley, Jr., April 16, 2015.

For early preceptresses see *College of Puget Sound Quarterly Bulletins*, 1914-1915 through 1917-1918 and *Tamanawas* 1923, p. 23.

Lyle's NYU study is mentioned in the October 1934 issue of *Puget Sound Alumnus*, p. 2; her degree in Puget Sound catalogs. Courses she taught are listed in Puget Sound Class Schedules spring 1949 through spring 1953.

See "Lyle Ford Drushel," by R. Franklin Thompson, "Thompson Histories, Portraits" (1900). University Historical Texts, Book 7.

Warren Everett Tomlinson, pages 153-161

Homer Maris' collision with the bicycle is documented in the October 2, 1933, issue of *The Trail*, as well as in the 1934 *Tamanawas*. See the transcript (online at Sound Ideas) of R. Franklin Thompson's April 23, 1979 interview with Warren Tomlinson. For a story about Professor Tomlinson and his role on campus, see "Tomlinson's Travels Told" in *The Trail*, October 31, 1947, p. 2. For Tomlinson's globetrotting ways, see *The Trail*, October 6, 1950 and "Globe Trotting German Instructor Added to Puget Sound Faculty," in *The Trail*, October 23, 1933. The "sizzle" story and more about Jeannette can be found in *Warren E. Tomlinson, some history*, by Tomlinson's daughter Vivian Tomlinson Williams at ancestry.com. Tomlinson's Hitler quote is found in "Tomlinson's Travels Told" in *The Trail*, October 31, 1947. Tomlinson's Korean War student survey results are reported in *The Trail*, February 19, 1952. The report on Professor Tomlinson's presentation at the October 2, 1951, convocation (chapel) appears in *The Trail*, October 5, 1951. For more on "the PTA lecture circuit" see *The Trail*, October 20, 1950. For a photograph of Professor Tomlinson and Professors John Phillips, Christian Miller, and Raymond Powell with the CPS banner they took with them to Sweden, see *The Trail*, May 16, 1952. Tomlinson's 1952 Southampton departure is documented at ancestry.com. Jeannette's passing is noted in *The Trail*, February 14, 1961.

Deep Creek Lodge, pages 163-177

I am grateful to Chuck Howe '50, '51 for sharing his collection of Deep Creek Lodge photographs and documents. These and his personal recollections made this story possible. Mr. Howe continued to ski well into his 80s. Important also were personal interviews with Frank Peterson '50 and Sally Sprenger. The story of Deep Creek Lodge, the Chinook Club, and their annual winter ski carnivals is documented in great detail in issues of *The Trail* between 1948 and 1957, and in photographs published in volumes of *Tamanawas* for those years. Many more Deep Creek photographs can be found online at A Sound Past. In addition, see R. Franklin Thompson's "Portrait of Dr. Robert Sprenger," in *R.F. Thompson Portraits*, ASC and online at Sound Ideas, 1980. See also "CPS Buys Winter Lodge Near Mount Rainier," in the College of Puget Sound *Alumnus*, December, 1948.

Sources

University Place: The Campus that Almost Was, pages 179-189
In hindsight it seems University Place should have worked. Understanding why it did not and why better management was not brought to bear on the project requires an effort to get into the minds of the men in charge. This made digging out the story of University Place a sometimes frustrating experience because there was no one person to kick in the pants over it. I had a better time when I accepted the fact that the campus we do have is one of the most beautiful and functional in the world, a reality that is far better than a dream, even if the dream is alluring.

Sources for the University Place story include Todd's *History of the College of Puget Sound*, pages 45, 126, 132, 134, 143, 146, and 148; the booklet *University Place, the Site of Puget Sound University,* published by University Land Company, Tacoma, 1895, available online at Sound Ideas; Puget Sound University Trustee Meeting Minutes, especially 1893-1894, not available online; the November 15 1895, December 15, 1895, and January 15, 1896, issues of the student newspaper *University Record,* available online at Sound Ideas; and the August 1898 and July 1899 issues of the student newspaper *Ye Recorde,* available online at Sound Ideas.

The University Land Company was incorporated at Olympia on April 26, 1894, and was stricken from the records at Olympia on August 23, 1909. See the letter from Secretary of State Belle Reeves about this, dated November 20, 1944, to Edward Todd ,that is attached to the April 17, 1894, trustee meeting minutes.

About architect George Wesley Bullard's Tacoma Congregational Church and University of Illinois Engineering Hall designs, see explorecu.org/items/show/279?tour=12&index=9#.VIX8cTHF_E0 and explorecu.org/tour-builder/tours/show/id/12#.VIX9nTHF_E0, respectively. Information about Bullard, in addition to the student newspaper sources listed above, may be found at digital.lib.washington.edu/architect/architects/4962.

The directive to merge Puget Sound University and Portland University came from a joint commission of the three Pacific Northwest conferences (Puget Sound, Columbia River, and Portland) of the Methodist Church. The commission was influenced primarily by the views of member Dr. C.H. Payne of New York. Elected secretary of the church's Board of Education, Payne favored consolidation of Methodist schools within each region of the country. Reluctant PSU trustees' came up with a resolution to merge as they were directed to do. The resolution specified that PSU and PU must submit a proposal to determine the merged college's location. Proposals were to be submitted by August 31, 1898, with the opening of school delayed until October 4. The proposals were to address five items: (1) payment of debt; (2) providing for protection of holders of lots sold to found and equip the schools (the Portland idea was to essentially use the University Place scheme of funding the school through the sale of lots at what is now the location of the University of Portland), (3) securing of buildings and equipment, (4) endowment and providing for running expenses, and (5) most advantageous location. PU did not address the five items to PSU's satisfaction, giving PSU trustees a way out of the merger. They complied with the church's directive to merge in a way that made the merger impossible under the circumstances (Portland University was in worse financial straits than Puget Sound). The site of the merged institution was to be land Portland University was attempting to acquire, at the location of today's University of Portland, a Catholic college having nothing whatsoever to do with the old Methodist college Portland University except that PU made the original effort to locate where UOP stands today.

Vienna 1966 and 50 Years of Study Abroad, pages 191-198
The 1966 Vienna Semester Abroad students are: Anne Alworth, Jo Baxter, Gary Birchler, Betty Blanchard, Steven Bradley, Elizabeth (Libby) Brown, Alexander (Al) Campbell, Gordon Cooke, Jean Crosetto, Charles Curran, Georgia Depue, Dianne (Dee Dee) Dressel, John Finney, Karen Finney, Jerianne Fopp, Peter Galloway, Diane Garland, Kay Hatfield, Mary Margaret Hillier, Alvah (Al) Howe, David Johnson, Rodney Johnson, John Johnston, Gerard Kern, Russell McCurdy, Janet McLellan, James Nelson, Victor Nelson, Lawrence Nicholson, Alan Nordell, Frank Osmanski, Larry Otto, Calmar (Cal) Peterson, Alexis Roberts, Douglas Smith, Robert Sprenger, Donald Taylor, David Wagner, Elizabeth (Liz) Watson, and Isa Werny.

The Methodist Connection, pages 199-201
John Magee was a Harvard Ph.D, a brilliant philosopher, and a calm, deliberative force on the campus. As a child, I remember John Magee visiting my family from time to time, and one time he brought me a rubber tomahawk. Perhaps it was supposed to be a toy hatchet, I'm not sure. The fact that John Magee taught at Puget Sound was one reason I applied for admission, and he was my first academic advisor. His office was then (1963) in South Hall, the former army hospital barracks razed in 2011. John Magee taught with an open, searching mind. One time in the 1960s my then-academic advisor, Professor of Sociology Frank Peterson, told me that a wealthy patron had promised President Thompson he would give to the college a large amount of money if Thompson would get rid of Magee, whom the patron believed was too liberal for a church school. Thompson refused, of course. John Magee was the major force that finally in 1985 brought a chapter of Phi Beta Kappa to the Puget Sound campus. I still miss John Magee. He helped to shape who and what we are today.

My Life as a Cold War Spy, pages 203-208
When I look back on this 1966 experience I am amazed at the degree to which World War II and even the 1956 Hungarian revolution seemed to be so far in the past to me then. Now I think of events 10 and 20 years ago and they are like yesterday. Yet the same is true of all generations of students. In Vienna, Professor Tomlinson assigned us the task of answering in writing this question: Could Nazism ever arise in Germany again? I wrote that of course it could not—that was then, the olden days, and this (1966) was

Sources

now, the modern days when such outrages were impossible by the natural progression of civilization that we children of the 1960s believed in. Tomlinson's comments on my paper consisted of a big question mark and "I'm not so sure." That made me think a little more about the question then and, over the years, a lot more about it.

Puget Sound Timeline, pages 215-237
See the basic references identified at the beginning of this Sources section. Specific comments and additional references are:

Presidents
Crawford Thoburn's dates are sometimes listed as 1892-1899 and Wilmot Whitfield's as 1899-1900. However, review of trustee minutes makes it clear that Wilmot Whitfield was elected president in December, 1898. At the same meeting, the decision was made to bring the school from Portland back to Tacoma and to begin classes on March 7, 1899. Thoburn never returned to Tacoma and had no further dealing with Puget Sound University. He took the pastorate at Centenary Methodist Church in Portland, dying there on May 9, 1899. Thus, more accurate dates are Crawford Thoburn 1892-1898 and Wilmot Whitfield 1898-1900.

Deans of Women
Margaret Walker's official title was associate dean of students and director of women's affairs. She had been dean of women at Pepperdine. At Puget Sound she fulfilled the role of dean of women, which title returned to the office with the hiring of Walker's successor, Mary Louise Curran, the last dean of women.

Historical Timeline
Two additional references are Professor Walter Davis' history of the college published in *Tamanawas* annually for several years beginning in 1921, and George Arney's "Side Lights on the History of the Puget Sound University and the University of Puget Sound as I Came in Contact With These Institutions," document 7 in *Volume of Miscellaneous Manuscripts written by Men who took part in the founding and early History of College of Puget Sound*, Volume I, University Archives Mss 034. See also, of course, Edward Todd's history of the college.

Greek Life
See the June 1926 issue of *The Trail* and the 1922 *Tamanawas* for descriptions of early sororities and fraternities.

UNIVERSITY OF PUGET SOUND | CAMPUS MAP

BUILDINGS

1. Alcorn Arboretum
2. Anderson/Langdon Residence Hal
3. Athletics and Aquatics Center
4. Baker Stadium/Peyton Field/ Shotwell Track
5. Baseball Diamond
6. Benefactor Plaza
7. Center for Intercultural and Civic Engagement
8. Ceramics Building
9. Commencement Walk
10. Communications House
11. East Athletic Field
12. Event Lawn
13. Expeditionary
14. Facilities Service
15. Harned Hall/Oppenheimer Café
16. Harrington Residence Hall
17. Howarth Hall
18. Human Resources
19. Jones Circle
20. Jones Hall/Norton Clapp Theatre
21. Karlen Quad
22. Kilworth Memorial Chapel
23. Kittredge Hall and Art Gallery
24. Langlow House
25. Library, Collins Memorial
26. Lower Baker Field
27. McIntyre Hall
28. Memorial Fieldhouse/Pamplin Sports Center
29. Music Building/Schneebeck Concert Hall
30. Oppenheimer Hall
31. President's House
32. Print and Copy Services
33. Regester Residence Hall
34. Schiff Residence Hall
35. Sculpture Building
36. Security Services
37. Seward Residence Hall
38. Smith Residence Hall
39. Softball Field
40. Student Activities/Residence Life
41. Student Diversity Center
42. Tennis Pavilion
43. Theme House Row
44. Thomas Hall
45. Thompson Hall
46. Todd Field
47. Todd/Phibbs Residence Hall
48. Trimble Residence Hall/ Trimble Forum
49. Union Avenue Residences
50. University Club
51. University of Puget Sound Garden
52. Warner Gymnasium
53. Weyerhaeuser Hall/Mobility Park
54. Wheelock Student Center/ Diversions Café/The Cellar/ Rasmussen Rotunda/Bookstore
55. Wyatt Hall

FORMER BUILDINGS KEY:

◆ South Hall
★ HR House
▲ A-Frames
○ First Hugh Wallace Memorial Pool
● Music Conservatory Bldg.

257